THE L DOWNUNDER

by Ted Egan

Preface by Rolf Harris

Grice Chapman
PUBLISHING

First published in the U.K. in 2003
by Grice Chapman Publishing
A subsidiary of Financial Television Ltd.
The Shire House
Burgh next Aylsham
Norwich
NR11 6TP

www.gricechapman.com

Text © Ted Egan 2003
Cover © Bob Marchant 2003

All rights reserved. No part of this publication may be reproduced, stored in a retrieval system or transmitted in any form or by any means, electronic, mechanical, photocopying, recording or otherwise, without the prior permission of the Copyright holder.

ISBN 0-9545726-0-2

British Library Cataloguing in Publication Data
A catalogue record for this book is available from the British Library.

Cover artwork by Bob Marchant, Bundeena,
New South Wales, Australia

Designed and printed by Barnwell's Print Ltd., Aylsham,
Norfolk, NR11 6ET, UK
tel: +44 (0) 1263 732767

PREFACE

I've known and admired Ted Egan for many years, in fact, since he suggested I should record a song he knew called *Two Little Boys*. He is a marvellous man, a great entertainer with a gift for communication. Ted's knowledge of and empathy for the people who have shaped our land, shines through in this book. It is 'everyman's' Australian history - one which will appeal to young and old alike.

As if the words were not enough to bring the story to life, we have the pleasure of listening to his songs. More than 25 songs, written and recorded by Ted, mirror the stories of the men and women we read about on these pages. I commend the whole project to anyone who wants to know more about - and get under the skin of - the Land Downunder.

Rolf Harris

Two Little Boys: Ted Egan introduces Rolf Harris to the song
Photo: Ted Egan

LIST OF SONGS

1. For the Terms of Their Natural Lives
2. Jim Jones at Botany Bay
3. A Bunch of Damned Whores
4. Mary: The Girl from Botany Bay
5. Benelong and The White Sea Eagle
6. Gurindji Blues
7. Brown Skin Baby
8. God's Police
9. Bullocky's Joy and Jesus
10. Rider in the Mirage
11. King Paraway
12. Old Ned
13. The Drover's Boy
14. Alyandabu
15. Drought
16. Granny
17. The Bush Woman
18. Marsupial Joe
19. The Anzacs
20. A Song for Grace
21. Beersheba
22. Greater Love Than This
23. The Union Way
24. The Tiger and The Don
25. Willy the Whinging Pom
26. I've Been Everywhere, Ma'am
27. She's Australian
28. This Land Australia

CONTENTS

INTRODUCTION		9
PROLOGUE		10
1	Back In The Old Dart	12
2	For The Terms Of Their Natural Lives	16
3	Jim Jones & Others At Botany Bay	24
4	A Bunch Of Damned Whores	30
5	Across The Seas To Freedom	38
6	Benelong & The White Sea Eagle	46
7	No Worse, There Is None	50
8	The First Australians	56
9	Land Rights: The Gentle Persuader	64
10	The Stolen Generation	78
11	Free Settlers: God's Police	88
12	The Sleepy Growth Of The Colonies	94
13	Explorers, Gold, Bushrangers, Eureka	102
14	Old Bluey & The Intrepid Scot	108
15	Overlanders, Drover's Boys, & Other Women Pioneers	120
16	Multi-Cultural Australia? Are You Fair Dinkum?	132
17	Mining: Boom & Bust	140
18	The Spirit Of ANZAC	148
19	Greater Love Than This: The Man With The Donkey	162
20	We'll Shear The Union Way	168
21	The Tiger & The Don	176
22	Try To Understand	192
23	Not Alien, Australian	214
GLOSSARY OF TERMS		223
RECOMMENDED READING LIST		229

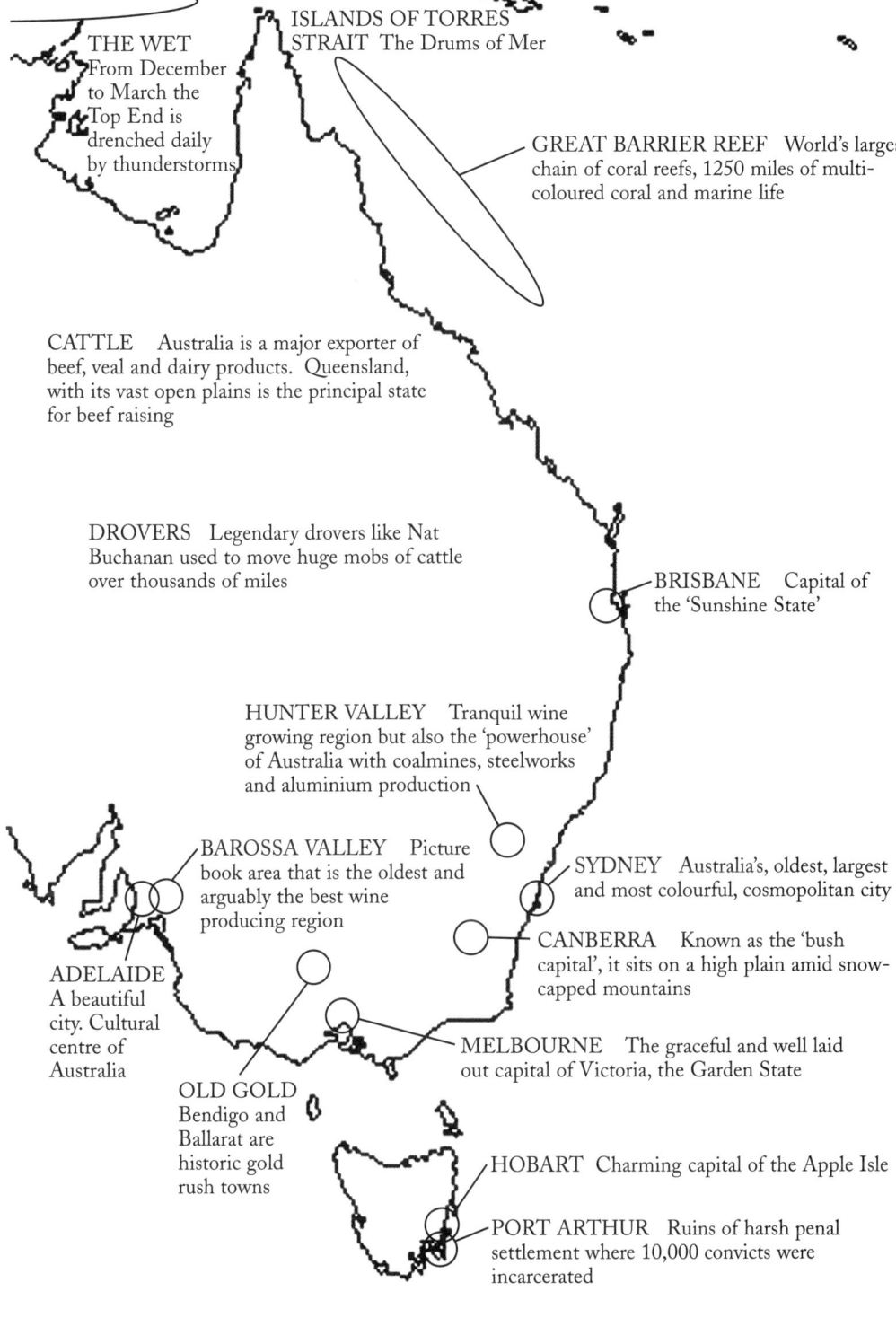

Dedication

*To all the people, the 'Faces of Australia', who inspired the songs.
For they created the history*

INTRODUCTION

Australia is an island continent, approximately equal in land area to the United States of America, ten times the area of Britain and Ireland. The population at commencement of the 21st century was slightly in excess of 20 million people, from many diverse backgrounds. Australia was colonised by the British in 1788, when a penal colony was established in New South Wales. The original Australians, the Aboriginals (referred to in this book as The First Australians) number around 500,000, based on their own identification.

In political terms the Commonwealth of Australia is an independent member of the Commonwealth of Nations. The Queen of England, Her Majesty Queen Elizabeth the Second, is also Queen of Australia. As such she is Australia's Head of State, represented in Australia by a Governor-General, six State Governors, and Administrators of the various Territories.

Australia has a Federal Parliament, six state and two Territory parliaments. The Federal Parliament sits in Canberra, the national capital. Parliament consists of the Lower (ruling) House, the House of Representatives; and the Upper House (states rights, house of review), the Senate.

There are six states of Australia - in descending order of population:
New South Wales (NSW), capital Sydney
Victoria (VIC), capital Melbourne
Queensland (QLD), capital Brisbane
South Australia (SA), capital Adelaide
Western Australia (WA), capital Perth
Tasmania (TAS) - an island state, capital Hobart

And two mainland Territories, both self-governing:
Northern Territory (NT), capital Darwin.
Australian Capital Territory (ACT) - location of the national capital, Canberra.

PROLOGUE

Mary Broad began to plan her daring escape after her husband William Bryant, was flogged for selling fish in exchange for rum. Governor Arthur Phillip had promised to be merciless to convicts and soldiers alike on two counts - proven theft of food, and ill-treatment of 'the Indians'. Phillip had already sentenced the seventeen year old convict Thomas Barrett to be hanged for stealing precious food from the Company store.

It was 1790. The British settlers had been at Port Jackson, New South Wales, for two years. They seemed resolved to starve, eking out an existence on stringently-rationed, rancid salt pork and weavilly flour. Attempts to grow English crops and vegetables had failed. The many colourful local birds ate the seeds as fast as they were planted. The British were still waiting for the Second Fleet to arrive from England with more 'real' foodstuffs. In their immediate vicinity, the Iora tribe of Aboriginals thrived on their protein-rich diet of oysters, fish, crayfish, prawns and kangaroo, supplemented by eggs, fruits, nuts, and berries in season.

Table D'Hôte, 1790

First Fleeters (officers, marines & sailors)	Iora Aboriginals
Mouldy bread	Sydney rock oysters, crayfish & prawns
Rancid salt pork and beef with turnip tops and dried peas	*Choice of:* Kangaroo served with roasted nuts and seeds, or Freshly caught grilled snapper
Preserved pears	Seasonal berries & fruits
Tot of rum	
Convicts: less of the above & no rum	Water

From the outset the newcomers felt the locals, the First Australians, had nothing of consequence to offer. There was land, of course, but the British knew that their legally valid doctrine of *terra nullius* allowed them to occupy this island continent with impunity. The natives displayed none of the normal signs denoting meaningful occupancy of land - there were no dwellings, no fences, no crops, no defence system. It was truly 'a land belonging to nobody'- a land bound to benefit from British civilisation and Christianity.

No one was given the task of learning the local language. There was no attempt to tap into the Aboriginals' age-old knowledge of this uncompromising, seemingly inhospitable land. Instead of marvelling at the lifestyle that enabled the Aboriginals to go naked, erect only the most rudimentary of shelters, and restrict their possessions to the simplest of weapons and utensils, the new arrivals saw only uncivilised, unclad savages - heathens, seemingly abandoned by Almighty God - who slept most of the day, and danced through the night.

Mary Broad knew what needed to be done. She had to get back to England at all costs. She began to plot one of the great escapes of world history.

Transportation to Botany Bay: convicts escape the gallows
Thomas Rowlandson's drawing by permission of the National Library of Australia
Rex Nan Kivell Collection

CHAPTER 1

Back In The Old Dart

> As one reads history one is absolutely sickened, not so much by the crimes the wicked have committed, but by the punishments the good have inflicted.
>
> Oscar Wilde

Prior to 1820 in Britain there was no penitentiary system as we know it today. There were simply gaols like Newgate, mediaeval cesspits of crime and disease, where prisoners were incarcerated, regardless of age or sex. There was no attempt to reform, but simply to punish the prisoners and remove them from sight.

Often gaols were privately owned and operated, and prisoners were required to pay for their food. One can only speculate on the ways in which this might, or might not, have been achieved.

Hundreds of offences earned the death penalty. As late as 1811 Bills seeking to have the death penalty waived for stealing goods valued at less than five shillings, were stubbornly rejected by the House of Lords. The ever-increasing crime rate provided obvious evidence that hanging was not an effective deterrent to crime. Nonetheless Lord Chancellor Eldon asserted:

> It is not the circumstances of the severity of the law being put into execution to the fullest extent, so much as the imaginary terrors of it which produces the abhorrence of crime.

From the middle of the eighteenth century many of those sentenced to death had their sentences commuted to

Botanist Joseph Banks proposed Botany Bay as a penal colony
William Dickinson portrait by permission of the National Library of Australia
Rex Nan Kivell Collection

transportation to the American colonies or the Caribbean plantations for 14 years. Lesser offences attracted seven years transportation.

There were two reasons for the eventual discontinuation of this practice. Firstly, the plantation owners turned more and more to the importation of African labour: 50,000 black slaves were sent to America in 1775. Second, in that same year the American Revolution took place, forcing Britain to look for other ways to rid herself of the 'criminal class.'

The British gaols were full, and stinking. Confident that the American uprising would soon be quashed, the British Parliament passed the *Hulks Act (1776)*. The overflow of prisoners now went to the many derelict hulks of old warships moored in rivers and at seaports and the prisoners were put to work on public tasks like road making and canal digging. This had previously been resisted. There was no shortage of labour, and the 'good people' did not derive any joy from being affronted by the sight of the criminal class. Now they locked their doors more securely and simply prayed to be rid of the felons.

Hopes of quelling the American insurgence diminished, so new and different solutions had to be found. Two options were considered: either the reformist penitentiary system advocated by Jeremy Bentham and others, or transportation to another place.

Initially no one was in a hurry to choose. Either alternative would obviously be expensive. But when the hulks were overflowing and the crime rate continued to spiral upwards something had to be done. Hesitantly, a momentous decision was taken.

In the face of considerable adverse logistical evidence it was decided to establish a penal colony at Botany Bay in New Holland, later to be called Australia. Botany Bay had been named and recommended by the botanist Joseph Banks, a member of the Cook expedition of 1770.

First Fleet Commander Captain Arthur Phillip brought the convicts to Sydney Cove, "one of the finest harbours in the world"
Portrait by Henry Macbeth-Raeburn by permission of the National Library of Australia

CHAPTER 2

For The Terms Of Their Natural Lives

> I sentence you, but to what I know not; perhaps to storm and shipwreck, perhaps to infectious disorders, perhaps to famine, perhaps to be massacred by savages, perhaps to be devoured by wild beasts. Away! Take your chance! Perish or prosper, suffer or enjoy. I rid myself of the sight of you.
>
> **Jeremy Bentham**

Bentham and other eighteenth century social reformers in Britain vehemently opposed transportation on the grounds that it was expensive, unproductive, and achieved nothing other than the removal of people who had offended society. Bentham proposed as an alternative that prisoners be isolated, made to work productively, subjected to discipline and given incentives. Parliament wanted none of it. Liberal, unrealistic, expensive nonsense, they said. Humbug.

The transportationists were obviously going to triumph, but it is nonetheless interesting to wonder why Australia eventually got the nod. Various places along the African coast would have seemed better choices. The convicts could be sent to Africa on slave-ships which could then ply their other human trade to the Americas. The convicts could be put to tasks like mining and their provisioning supplied by ships of the East India Company sailing to and fro around the Cape of Good Hope. Every African, and other, option was considered by Parliament in detail, yet the choice was still Botany Bay. Why?

Was it to be just a penal colony, a place of no return? It has subsequently been suggested that it was a clever strategic move to set up an outpost of Empire deterring the French, Dutch and others from any future actions relating to India and South East Asia, known at the time as the East Indies. If this was the case, surely the First Fleet would have been better equipped? Surely some tradespeople would have been sent? Some farmers, perhaps? And even though there were contemporaneous designs on Norfolk Island, its impressive pine trees and (supposedly) large areas of flax, no ships artificers were sent with the First Fleet.

One of the great delusions beautifully perpetrated to this day by the English is that if people are called Lord So and So, or Earl Such and Such, the bearer of the title is thereby a wise and clever person, naturally making learned, rational, noble - if you like - decisions. But the First, Second and Third Fleets,

Goodbye forever: Black-eyed Sue and Sweet Poll of Plymouth part from their lovers, bound for Botany Bay
Robert Sayer engraving by permission of the National Library of Australia
Rex Nan Kivell Collection

victualled and organised by the enobled decision makers in the Home and Colonial Office to transport 5,000 people to Australia between 1787 and 1791, were totally ill-equipped and incredibly unprepared for what lay ahead of them on the other side of the world.

The newly-appointed Governor of New Holland, as the penal colony was first known, was also the Commander of the First Fleet, Captain Arthur Phillip. He constantly but unsuccessfully urged his superiors to provide generous supplies of clothing, medicines and anti-scorbutics. Because of Phillip's personality and persistence, the First Fleet was better supervised and fitted out than the disastrous Second and Third Fleets, which were let out to private shipping contractors. But even the First Fleet suffered unnecessarily and severely because of the pig-headedness of Phillip's superiors who arrogantly felt that, being British, they could organise expeditions anywhere.

Convicts were crammed between decks on the transport ships, which had extra bulkheads and barriers, fitted with loopholes through which the soldiers could shoot if necessary. The decks were crowded with livestock, and the holds of the storeships were packed with the supplies and foodstuffs meant to last for the voyage plus an anticipated two years.

The First Fleet, with 717 convicts guarded by 191 marines and 19 officers, crossed the Atlantic Ocean twice, revictualling at Rio de Janiero before arriving at Cape Town on 13 October 1787. Here Captain Phillip bought more provisions and livestock; and he transferred from HMS *Sirius* to HMS *Supply* which had established itself as the faster of the two escort ships. *Supply* entered Botany Bay on 18 January 1788. Phillip was dismayed to see the low, sterile, featureless coastline. When, 18 years earlier in 1770, Captain Cook had landed at Botany Bay it was May and late autumn. There had been good rains and he and Banks had enthused about 'green meadows'. Here was Phillip in Antipodean mid-summer, seeing the land either brown and parched, or recently burnt black by Aboriginal hunters. While waiting for the other ships to arrive Phillip sailed north in *Supply*, to discover, to his pleasant surprise, a harbour where "a thousand ships of the line" could safely shelter. He immediately contemplated a change of location for the penal colony. On 26 January 1788 Phillip came ashore at a place in the harbour that would be called Sydney Cove, later, simply Sydney. It was thus named to honour Thomas Townshend, Viscount Sydney, the inept, obtuse Home and Colonial Secretary who had done so much to frustrate Phillip's preparations. Nobody thought to check that the traditional Iora name for the area was *Warung*.

The convicts transported on the First, Second and Third Fleets would scarcely have been impressed had they known that, back in England, the more strident critics of transportation asserted that felons were now placed as "their own masters in a temperate climate, where they have every object of comfort for ambition before them". Thus thundered Alexander Dalrymple, in his *Serious Admonition to the Public on the Intended Thief Colony at Botany Bay*. And *The Whitehall Post* put it in verse. It was a shame, they felt, that convicts would:

> Go to an island to take special charge,
> Much warmer than Britain, and ten times as large;
> No custom-house duty, no freightage to pay,
> And tax-free they'll live when at Botany Bay.

The voyages, as far as the convicts were concerned, resembled hell on earth (or water), especially the Second and Third Fleets. In *The Fatal Shore*, Robert Hughes describes in detail the horrors of these voyages. In the Second Fleet the slave-trade contractors Camden, Calvert and King were engaged to transport the male convicts @ £17-7-6 (£17.37p) per head, regardless of whether the prisoners arrived alive or not. The convicts were put into the shackles usually reserved for the shorter journey of slaves from West Africa to America. The ships leaked badly and the prisoners were cheated of their meagre rations to the point of absolute starvation. The inaccurate records indicate that around 1200 convicts sailed from England in the Second Fleet, including over 200 women on the *Lady Juliana*. Two hundred and sixty seven convicts died during the voyage. Another 150 died in the three months after arrival. The British authorities had simply cleared the prison hulks to supply the numbers for the Second Fleet, with no

Life below deck on an emigrant ship in 1850 was a different world from that experienced by the convicts in the late 18th century.

regard for age or health standards. The contractors no doubt felt that they were doing society a favour as they threw the cadavers overboard. The first thing they did on arrival at Sydney was to sell at exorbitant prices the food and clothing left over. The starving First Fleeters had no option but to pay the prices sought.

Later voyages are also described, like that of *Britannia* which sailed in 1796 from Cork in Ireland with 144 male and 44 female Irish on board, under Captain Thomas Dennett. The captain feared mutiny and proceeded to thrash six convicts to death. One man, James Brannon, received 800 lashes in 48 hours and died several days later. Altogether 7,000 lashes were administered. A subsequent inquiry found that Dennett's actions "bordered on too great a degree of severity". This was surely one of the more memorable bureaucratic whitewashes.

Although songs about Botany Bay are full of tooral-ay-adadees, ideal for a school pageant, they tell us little about the horrors of getting to the place. Nor do they point to the quite calculated and arguably sinister decision-making processes of the ruling classes in England. The first newspaper ever published in Australia, *The New Holland Morning Post* of 18 October 1791 carried this article:

> **Convicts Must Remain With Us**
>
> His Majesty's Government has made it plain it does not want the convicts back in England's shores, and has instructed Governor Phillip not to encourage them to return once they are emancipated.

So in every case convicts sentenced to seven years, 14 years, or life, were in fact banished from their homeland and their families for the terms of their natural lives. Perhaps the rich and privileged thought they would eventually have a crime-free society in Britain.

For The Terms Of Their Natural Lives

My Lords and my Ladies
I crave your attention
I speak on the subject of crime.
There's far too much of it
And those who commit it
Are surely the curse of our time.

We gentry and good folk
Just can't be affronted
By all of these felons and crooks:
And robbers and poachers
And harlots and varlets
And swindlers who fiddle the books.

They're awful, they're vicious,
They're excrementitious,
They're scum, and a damn they're not worth.
So I put it to you,
This verminous crew
Should be banned from the land of their birth.

To the faraway ends of the earth
We will send them-
A truly ingenious plan.
For the terms of their natural lives
We'll transport them.
We'll send them as far as we can.

CHORUS
Send them away to Botany Bay.
It's a truly ingenious plan.
For the terms of their natural lives
We will send them.
We'll send them as far as we can.
Send them away to Botany Bay,
A truly ingenious plan
For the terms of their natural lives
We will send them.
We'll send them as far as we can.

The hulks and the prisons
Are full to the brim
With criminals all doing time.
Hanging's much better,
But terribly messy
And doesn't deter them from crime.

And now we have all of
These liberal thinkers
Who tell us to find a new way.
But surely the only
Commitment we have
Is to show them that crime doesn't pay.

CHORUS
Send them away etc.

Then we gentle good folk
Can start to enjoy
The rich life we really deserve.
For Lord only knows
It's our God-given right,
Our truly blue-blooded preserve.

So none of this nonsense
Of all being equal
And meek who'll inherit the earth.
Let's once and for all
Give the criminal class
The treatment we reckon they're worth.

CHORUS
Send them away etc.

After eight long months at sea, convict ship Surry arrives in Sydney Harbour
Geoffrey Ingleton etching by permission of the National Library of Australia

CHAPTER 3

Jim Jones & Others At Botany Bay

> **They'll flog the poaching hide off you Down there at Botany Bay**
>
> *Jim Jones*, anon.

Although Captain Phillip decided to settle at Sydney Cove, in Port Jackson, the perception in Britain and Europe was that the penal colony was located at Botany Bay, as originally planned. It was referred to as such in much European correspondence until the 1830s, by which time there were stations holding convicts at Sydney, Port Macquarie, Newcastle, (New South Wales), Van Diemen's Land (Tasmania), Norfolk Island, Swan River (Western Australia), Moreton Bay (Queensland), Port Phillip (Victoria), and Fort Dundas on the Arafura Sea (Northern Territory).

When Phillip landed at Botany Bay on 18 January 1788, he officially became Governor of New South Wales. He was interested in the local Aboriginals, and made reasonably solicitous contact with them - at first. They in turn were fascinated by these strange creatures sweltering in their hot uniforms, although the marines were not required to show their genitalia, as had happened on Cook's visit. After exploring Port Jackson with Lieutenant John Hunter, Phillip returned to Botany Bay with exciting news about the new location. Then, to their amazement, two French ships under the command of the French explorer Jean François de la Perouse, also sailed into Botany Bay. The next morning, 26 January 1788, Phillip left Hunter to parley with La Perouse and he sailed quickly to Port Jackson to symbolise their arrival and occupation by raising the flag.

Relationships with La Perouse were quite cordial. He stayed at Botany Bay for six weeks before sailing off into the Pacific. The Frenchman was drowned later near the New Hebrides.

Australians recognise 26 January as Australia Day, but it was not until 7 February 1788 that the ceremonial reading of the Royal Instructions took place and Phillip was sworn in as Governor. Perhaps, in true Australian style, that day should be observed as Hangover Day. On the previous day, the women convicts came ashore and the local Iora tribe was shown that 'civilisation' had truly arrived. Rum and fornication were the order of the day and night and it was a sick, sorry, motley crew who undertook the onerous but necessary pomp and circumstance of raising the flag, firing a volley and giving three hearty British cheers for His Majesty King George III. Thus was New South Wales launched on that sticky February morning.

History shows that the convicts could have had worse commanders than Arthur Phillip. He was a highly organised, well-intentioned and generally honourable man who, from the outset, envisaged the settlement would become a valued part of the Empire, rather than merely a costly outpost of incarceration. He set to work the most unskilled group of people imaginable (even had they been willing) on the task of building their own concentration camp in this most inhospitable land.

February is definitely Sydney's worst month. It is usually hot, humid, mosquito-ridden and subject to violent electrical storms, so one can imagine the levels of sullen despondency as the Empire-builders swung into action.

The timber was as hard as steel and prone to split and crack. The land was unproductive to say the least. The soil seemed generally sterile. The bugs and birds ate the seeds as fast as they were planted. At first, only simple wattle and daub huts were constructed but gradually, as a lime kiln was built and bricks of a type were manufactured, the little settlement began to take shape.

As instructed, Phillip immediately dispatched Lieutenant Phillip Gidley King (later the fourth Governor of New South Wales) to Norfolk Island with 22 people, some of them hand-picked convicts. They were told to start farms and gardens and generally explore the feasibility of using Norfolk Island pine for ships masts and the native flax for sails.

Back at Sydney Cove those convicts who worked hard and obeyed the rules settled into a reasonably disciplined routine. Phillip made it quite clear that he would be totally ruthless on two counts: stealing food, or ill-treating 'the Indians'. On the first count he quickly made an example of seventeen-year-old Thomas Barrett, who became the first person hanged in the colony, for stealing butter, peas and pork. On the second count he exacerbated the incipient hatred the convicts felt for the Aboriginals by invariably (at the outset) taking the side of the indigenous people. Phillip sincerely wished the Aboriginals to "have a high opinion of their new guests". Three years later, the bewildered Governor demanded "heads in bags" when Aboriginals speared a soldier named McIntyre.

Those Iora who did not quickly succumb to the white man's introduced diseases like cholera, smallpox and typhus remained hard-gutted on the abundance of marine and other foodstuffs they had always enjoyed in their bountiful environment. The newcomers persisted in their efforts to grow English-style crops as they ate the precious rations they had brought with them.

The great Australian institution of B.Y.O was introduced at this hungry time. 'Bring your own bread' was an automatic adjunct to every invitation issued among the families of the soldiers and guards. By 1790 the entire settlement would be on the verge of starvation on the shores of a marine Garden of Eden.

Jim Jones at Botany Bay

Oh listen for a moment lads,
And hear me tell my tale-
How o'er the sea from England's shore
I was condemned to sail.
The jury says, 'He's guilty, sir,'
And says the Judge, says he-
'For life, Jim Jones, I'm sending you
Across the stormy sea.'

'And take my tip, before you ship
To join an iron gang,
Don't be too gay in Botany Bay,
Or else you'll surely hang-
Or else you'll surely hang,' says he
'And after that, Jim Jones,
High upon the gallows tree
The crows will pick your bones.'

'You'll have no chance for mischief there,
Remember what I say,
They'll flog the poaching hide off you
Down there at Botany Bay.'

For night and day our irons clang
And like poor galley slaves
We toil and toil, and when we die
Must fill dishonoured graves.
But bye and bye, I'll break my chains
And to the bush I'll go.
I'll join the bold bushrangers there-
Jack Donahue and Co.

And late at night when everything
Is quiet in the town,
I'll kill the tyrants one and all,
I'll shoot the bastards down:
I'll give the law a little shock;
Remember what I say,
They'll yet regret they sent Jim Jones
In chains to Botany Bay.

"...we never wear drawers and they say we're the cause of dissension".
The Flash Mob at the Cascades Factory, Tasmania
By permission of Caroline Williams

CHAPTER 4

A Bunch Of Damned Whores

No, no - surely not! My God - not more of those damned whores! Never have I known worse women!"

Lt. Ralph Clark, of the First Fleet.

Ann Summers' book *Damned Whores and God's Police* is arguably the most important book ever written about Australia. The book studies attitudes towards Australian women, not just by men but by women themselves, about themselves. She writes:

> The traditional Judaeo-Christian notion that all women could be categorised as being exclusively either good or evil - with the Virgin Mary and Mary Magdalene being the prototypes of each kind - was brought to Australia with the First Fleet. But its application to the women of this country was totally lopsided. From 1788 until the 1840's almost all women were categorized as whores - or 'damned whores' as Lt. Ralph Clark called them.

Various writers have attempted to assess the percentage of prostitutes among the women transported to Australia, but while this is an interesting academic exercise it has little relevance to the ultimate fate of the women. The only conclusion that can be reached is that every single transported woman became a mere sexual object, subject to rape and every conceivable form of exploitation. It was not whoredom or prostitution, for most whores and prostitutes get paid for their services and may have a right of refusal. A convict woman had little option but to become the mistress and chattel of a particular man who would perhaps protect her as he might protect a horse, or a gun, from being stolen by another. This in turn often meant ongoing violence for the women if their proprietary male happened himself to be jealous or violent, or both.

Dr. Summers attributed Lieutenant Clark's remarks to a sighting of the *Lady Juliana*, a ship of the Second Fleet which brought over 200 female convicts to Sydney on 3 June 1790. Clark continually ranted about the actual or alleged morals of female convicts in his journal, which was dedicated to his beloved wife in England, Betsy Alicia. He neglected to record that a convict, Mary Branham, bore his illegitimate child on Norfolk Island.

The most sinister aspect was that this exploitation and denigration of women was a calculated part of the transportation system. Summers called the British government 'Imperial whoremasters'.

Phillip had ignored the section of his Instructions which suggested that he might "take aboard some women from the islands in those seas". He felt that the island women would "pine away in misery". He did, however, ask for more female convicts, though only to gratify the sexual passions of his soldiers, guards and (given a surplus) the convicts. He did not envisage that women would become a valuable part of the workforce.

Invariably the transported women came from poor, deprived backgrounds. Many women in Britain and Ireland had been forced to resort to stealing and prostitution simply in order to live. Among the male convicts there were many from privileged backgrounds who had committed crimes like perjury, fraud, or who were transported for other devious social misdemeanours. There is no record of any 'upper class' women being transported.

Both in the hulks and on the transport ships, the female convicts were sorted over by the soldiers, guards and crew. The optimum fate was to be chosen by a man relatively kind and sufficiently influential. Ann Ilett, who was chosen by Lt. Philip

Gidley King was one of the fortunate but even she was cast aside when King was ready to bring out his wife from England.

In the First Fleet a pattern was established. Women were there solely for the taking until the 1840s and even later when free female migrants were similarly accosted, and treated worse on arrival than convicts.

A later Governor, Lachlan Macquarie received a letter in 1809 from a settler named Plummer:

> It will perhaps scarcely be believed that, on the arrival of a female convict ship, the custom has been to suffer the inhabitants of the colony each to select one at his pleasure, not only as servants, but as avowed objects of intercourse.

Macquarie determined to make some changes. Viscount Castlereagh, Secretary of State for Colonies, did a paperwork *volte-face* when he instructed Macquarie, on behalf of His Majesty's Imperial Government:

> It has been represented to me that upon the arrival of female convicts in New South Wales, the unfortunate females have been given into the possession of such of the inhabitants, free settlers and convicts indiscriminately, as made a demand for them from the Governor. You will take the proper means for having the female convicts, upon their arrival, kept separate until they can be properly distributed in such a manner as may best encourage attention to industry and character.

Late in his term Macquarie was to commission the construction of the Parramatta Factory where, purportedly, women were protected while at the same time employed. But he was unable to beat the entrenched attitude that women were mere sexual chattels. Women were expected to pay for their accommodation at the Factory - and at the other workhouses established at Launceston and Hobart - but in many cases there was no work available to them, so they had no option but to sell their sexual services. This in turn led to corruption among those staffing the factories. A woman named Gordon, matron at Parramatta, is reputed to have made a fortune out of selling the women in her charge.

One of the few people to talk any sense on behalf of the female convicts was Lady Jane Franklin, the wife of an early Governor of Van Diemen's Land. Lady Franklin was a follower of the great Norfolk-born reformer Elizabeth Fry, who had done so much in England to alleviate the plight of the women being transported. Lady Franklin did not necessarily seek to reform those women who were inherently bad. She advocated education and better food and clothing in order that all women be given a chance to improve themselves.

Lady Jane Franklin worked hard to improve the lot of convict women. This did not go down well in London.
By permission of the State Library of Tasmania

Some of the women were indeed tough eggs. One group at the Cascades Factory in Tasmania was called *The Flash Mob*. They delighted in baring their backsides and smacking their buttocks in unison, to show their derision or displeasure, especially when bored by the sermons of clergymen who urged them to repent their wicked ways.

The lot of female convicts did not improve even after their sentences had been served. It was never possible to attain respectability, as men could. Those women who had married were deemed to have been 'saved' by marriage, but not made honourable. In the days when people wanted to forget 'the convict stain' women were often despised by their own children. It was the classic example of 'give a dog a bad name'. The noted bigot, the Reverend Samuel Marsden, known as the Flogging Parson, drew up the official Female Register in which women were placed in only two categories - married or concubine. His report was accepted in England as an accurate reflection of colonial morality.

Flogging of females was nowhere near as common as for males, although Marsden in his capacity as magistrate, sometimes ordered a flogging. On Norfolk Island, Foveaux 'The Tyrant' took perverse delight in having female convicts stripped naked and flogged in front of the assembled male convicts. At all times female convicts were subjected to the degrading attention of lascivious males, particularly those in positions of authority within the convict system. A feature of Foveaux's time as Commandant at Norfolk Island was the regular Thursday night dance, when the female convicts were stripped naked, filled up with rum, and required to perform the 'dance of the mermaids' for the soldiers. They had numbers painted on their backs and were given points for performance. Some traditions are slow to vanish. In recent years moronic, drunken 'hoons' in Bay 13 at the Melbourne Cricket Ground have kept the tradition alive by holding up cards giving points out of ten for any woman foolish enough to walk amongst them.

The 'God's Police' in Summers' title refers to the single girls brought to Australia as assisted migrants, notably by Caroline Chisholm, who believed that marriage, especially to Catholic girls, and family life were the best means of creating a

Caroline Chisholm founded Australia's first women's refuge in 1835. During the 1840s she cared for over 11,000 women and children in Sydney. Her face featured on the $5 note for 20 years.

quiescent, law-abiding male population.

The stereotypes remain today in the minds of many Australians, male and female, who believe that women are either good or bad, damned whores or God's police. Among Australian males there are still many who will savagely attack anyone who swears in front of their wives or daughters, but who themselves will reel off the most objectionable language imaginable in front of female bar staff in a pub. The rationale is that 'the woman I chose' or 'the girls I fathered' are necessarily good women, whereas women like barmaids are loose and generally out to lead a man astray.

Around the campfires of the Australian frontier it was always insisted that women were to be put on a pedestal. While this encouraged a code of politeness and shyness with white women, to the point of being embarrassingly funny, it allowed many of the same men to abuse, ravage and exploit Aboriginal women with impunity, absolute contempt and ferocity. They were there for the taking. They were never referred to as women. There always had to be a derogatory term like 'gin' or 'stud' or 'black velvet'. To use a very mixed metaphor, they were 'fair game'.

A Bunch of Damned Whores

CHORUS
We're a bunch of damned whores
And we never wear drawers
And they say we're the cause of dissension.
But none of your fuss
Before you judge us,
There's a few things that we'd like to mention.

Me name's Molly Brown
And the beak sent me down
For nickin' a gentleman's watch in The Strand.
So I'm sailin' away
From Southampton today.
Transported for life to Van Diemen's Land.

So if I'm one of them whores
And I never wears drawers,
It's simply that I can't afford 'em.
But it seems plain to me
That the English gentry
Is the baskets what causes the whoredom.

I'm Morag McDonald,
Born in the Gorbals
And raised in a brothel since I was aged ten.
And now I'm transported
For life for me sins
And they've handed me over to the Government men.

I wonder how just
It all is for I must
Now submit to the evils of this cruel lot.
They'll flog us and rape us
And tell us we're evil,
But they are the sinners- we're not.

CHORUS:- We're a bunch etc.

I'm Brigid O'Rourke
And I'm from County Cork;
A prisoner for life just for stealing a sheep
To feed me old parents
Who were squealin' with hunger.
Oh, Jesus, these times are so hard I could weep.

For I'm here in the Factory
Out at Parramatta,
And I'm sold to the soldiers and guards
By a dirty old harlot
Who takes all the money
And spends it on liquor and cards.

My name's Megan Rhys
I got nabbed by the police
In the back streets of Cardiff for pinching a dress.
I'm only eighteen
And I've been treated mean.
My life's been a story of unhappiness.

Drummed out of my parish
For having a child,
Whose father was killed in the war.
I was driven to vice,
So "Twll dîn, pob saes"
It's the system what made me a whore.

So lift up your skirts, girls,
And show your bare bums,
And slap on your buttocks me whorey old chums.
Let's show 'em we know 'em
For just what they are.
They're the world's greatest bastards by far.

*"So with my husband William,
And seven convict mates,
We stole a boat and sneaked it out to sea ..."*
The six-oared cutter headed north through the mountainous seas of
the Pacific Ocean to what is now Indonesia, 3,500 miles distant.

CHAPTER 5

Across The Seas To Freedom

> In Australia it was easy to escape.
> The hard thing was to survive.
>
> Robert Hughes, *The Fatal Shore*

'Done a bolt.' 'Shot through like a bolt.' The slang survives in Australia, harking back to the convict days when those who escaped were colloquially called bolters. Particularly among the Irish convicts transported in the First and Second Fleets, there was a belief that inland and northward from Port Jackson there was a large, traversable river which separated New Holland from China. It was not long before the first escapees tried their luck.

In attempting to escape overland, they either perished or were speared by Aboriginals. David Collins, Judge Advocate-cum-historian, reported on the numbers of skeletons to be seen between Port Jackson and Botany Bay. Some of the optimistic escapees carried a cardboard facsimile of a compass with the cardinal points marked thereon, but alas, no needle to point north.

Gradually the word filtered through that escape inland was pointless, even if achievable. On 26 September 1790 five convicts at Rose Hill, near Parramatta, stole a punt, rowed to Port Jackson where they appropriated a boat with a mast and sail, and put out to sea. They reached Port Stephens and four of them survived there for five years until 1795, when they were recaptured.

Over the next 50 years in the eastern states, many attempts at escape by sea were made by convicts, often assisted by American whaling captains who delighted in taking a tilt at the English. The crews of English transports would sometimes be sympathetic and stow convicts on their ships, in crannies unknown even to their officers.

In 1830 ten convicts from Sarah Island in Tasmania stole the 120 tonne brig *Frederick*, which they had built. They reached South America, but four of them were arrested and returned to Australia.

And then there was Mary Broad. Hers is surely one of the great escape and survival stories of all time. A sailor's daughter, she was baptised at Fowey, Cornwall, on 1 May 1765. On 20 March 1786 at Exeter Assizes she was sentenced to be hanged for stealing 'a bonnet and other goods' from Agnes Lakeman at Plymouth. The sentence was commuted to transportation for seven years. At first she was incarcerated on the hulk *Dunkirk*, in the English Channel off Plymouth. A year later she was transferred to the transport ship *Charlotte*, which sailed with the First Fleet on 13 May 1787. On the *Dunkirk* and the *Charlotte*, Broad teamed up with three male convicts, William Bryant, James Martin and James Cox. During the voyage to Australia she was 'delivered of a fine girl' who was baptized Charlotte, named either after the ship, or the reigning Queen of England, or both.

Broad landed at Port Jackson on 6 February 1788. Four days later she and Bryant were among the first five couples to be married European-style in Australia. As the convicts did not believe that their marriages would be legal back in England, she continued to refer to herself as Mary Broad rather than Bryant. Mary is the Dabby Bryant of Thomas Keneally's fine historical novel *The Playmaker*, which covers the production of *The Recruiting Officer*, the first stage play ever performed in Australia. It was directed by Lt. Ralph Clark.

Bryant was a Cornish fisherman who had been transported for smuggling. He was employed by Governor Phillip as the official fisherman. As such he was accorded privileges, amongst them a hut and the services of other convicts to grow his vegetables. Bryant succumbed to the temptation to trade fish for rum and he was given 100 lashes for his misdemeanour.

The Bryants began to plan their escape after word reached Port Jackson of the epic voyage of Captain Bligh in the launch of the *Bounty*. In 1791 Watkin Tench wrote, "After the escape of Captain Bligh, no length of passage, or hazard of navigation seemed above human accomplishment."

The runaways sneaked away from Benelong Point on the night of 28 March 1791. The party consisted of Mary Broad and her two babies, Emmanuel, twelve months, and Charlotte, three and a half years, William Bryant, James Martin and six other men. Their timing was impeccable. It was a dark, moonless night. HMS *Sirius* had sunk at Norfolk Island. HMS *Supply* had sailed to Norfolk Island six days earlier. The Dutch ship *Waaksamheyd*, whose skipper had supplied the convicts with a quadrant, compass, chart, ammunition and muskets, had sailed east to Europe via Cape Horn that very morning. Having avoided the scrutiny of the lookout at South Head, the Bryants and friends headed their little six-oared cutter out into the Pacific Ocean with the goal of reaching the island of Timor to the north west of Australia, 3,500 miles away. What a journey!

James Martin subsequently wrote his *Memorandoms* as an account of the voyage. They sailed and rowed through mountainous seas and treacherous reefs, once being three weeks at sea without daring to land. They endured searing heat and in the Torres Strait they had to row away from canoes full of fierce warriors they correctly identified as cannibals.

For a while, the journey became more peaceful. It was the ideal time to be crossing the Arafura Sea, with favourable south east winds driving their little craft under sail. They replenished their fresh water supply in Arnhem Land, and raced on to Coupang (Koepang), arriving on 5 June 1791. They had covered the 3,500 miles in 69 days and all hands were alive and well. William Morton, the navigator, had done a superb job.

When he saw a woman and two babies in the party, Governor Timotheus Wanjon readily believed their story that they were survivors from a sunken whaler. "As mariners in need of succour and support Governor Wanjon behaved extremely well to us, filled our bellies, and clothed double with everything that was wore on the island", wrote Martin.

It is likely that William Bryant's propensity for alcohol was again his undoing. It seems that he got drunk and, as Martin writes, "...had words with his wife, then went and informed against himself, wife and children, and all of us...We was immediately taken prisoners and was put in the castle."

Good fortune was now to abandon the party completely. The infamous Captain Edward Edwards was himself the survivor of a shipwreck. His ship, HMS *Pandora*, which had been used to round up some of the *Bounty* mutineers, arrived at Koepang on 17 September 1791. Edwards, a cold, hard man, devoid of sympathy and understanding, was informed, says Martin, "that we was convicts and had made our escape from Botany Bay. He told us we was his prisoners". Edwards chartered a Dutch ship, *Rembang* to take his entire group of prisoners from Koepang to the port of Batavia, prior to returning them to England.

Little Emmanuel Bryant died of fever at Batavia on 1 December 1791, aged 20 months. Exactly three weeks later, just before Christmas, his father William also succumbed to the fever. Batavia was living up to its reputation as the 'Golgotha of the East', a place reputed to kill off its entire European population every five years. The stagnant water was considered to be the problem.

At Batavia Edwards chartered four Dutch ships to Cape Town, where he found HMS *Gorgon* moored, en route from Port Jackson to England. Edwards decided to "avail myself of the opportunity to sail on her, with the ten pirates for England and the convict deserters from Port Jackson".

There were sharp reminders of convict times, for *Gorgon's* decks were crowded with 'kangaroos, opossums and every curiosity that country produced'. Also on board were Lt. Ralph Clark, of 'damned whores' notoriety and Captain Watkin Tench, modest and unassuming, 'that candid and liberal mind', whose observations during four years spent in Australia were both acute and astute.

Tench was greatly moved when he saw Mary Broad and the four survivors of the great escape. "I never looked at these people without pity and astonishment. They had miscarried in a heroic struggle for liberty, after having combated every hardship, and conquered every difficulty", he recorded. On 6 May 1792, Lt. Clark wrote the final chapter to Mary's *via dolorosa*: "Last night the child (Charlotte) belonging to Mary Broad, the convict woman who went away in the fishing boat from Port Jackson last year, died, about four o'clock. Committed the body to the deep."

The celebrated diarist James Boswell heard of the astonishing story of Mary Bryant (née Broad) and had her pardoned. He supported her financially for the rest of her life.
Portrait by George Dance by permission of the National Portrait Gallery, London

Mary returned to her homeland on 18 June 1792 to find herself not only a prisoner of the Crown, but one liable to capital punishment for escaping from lawful custody. Fortunately, Magistrate Nicholas Bond was sympathetic. Though he committed Broad and her four companions to Newgate Prison he promised to assist them. The court case attracted considerable public interest, and Broad was romantically dubbed 'Mary, the Girl From Botany Bay'.

James Boswell, biographer of Dr. Johnson, read of the escape and its aftermath. This zealous and literate man took up the defence of the escapees with typical tenacity. Boswell hounded Secretary of State Henry Dundas relentlessly, until finally, on 2 May 1793, 'Mary Bryant, otherwise Broad' was given an unconditional pardon. Her original seven-year sentence had expired six weeks earlier. Boswell settled an annual annuity of ten pounds on Mary Broad. She left London on what was to be her last voyage, sailing from the Thames, near Tower Hill, to Cornwall. The last record of her is acknowledging receipt of £5 at Lostwithiel on 1 November 1794. At that time she was 29 years old.

Martin's *Memorandoms* went to Jeremy Bentham, the English philosopher and social reformer, and they were not discovered until 1937.

The Girl from Botany Bay

Sitting by my window,
In a little fishing village
Back in Cornwall once again,
I reflect upon the time
I was put in chains and irons
When I stole a lady's bonnet,
And they sent me to Australia for my crime.

To deny the soldiers' lust
I placed my body and my trust
In the hands of William Bryant
Sent with me across the sea.
He'd been put away for smuggling,
So the two of us were shipped
To an unknown fate, an-unknown destiny.

I was married at Port Jackson.
I had two little children,
But life there was so dreadful
I formed a desperate plan.
I determined to escape
When my husband got a flogging,
And that's how my great adventure all began.

I'd heard how Captain Bligh
Had crossed the South Pacific Ocean,
Cast adrift by Fletcher Christian
In the Bounty mutiny.
So with my husband William,
And seven convict mates,
We stole a boat and sneaked it out to sea.

CHORUS
Sail
Across the dark and stormy ocean
To a destiny unknown and far away.
Sail
Across the seas to freedom
I'm Mary, the girl from Botany Bay.

Up the east coast of Australia
In the flimsy little craft,
Through storms and jagged coral,
In the treacherous Barrier Reef;
Three thousand miles of torment
Shielding my two little babies
From the hardships, which all seemed beyond belief.

We came ashore at Koepang
And were greeted by the Dutch.
And the Governor believed my tale,
That we'd been lost at sea.
But stupid William Bryant
Hit the rum and blew the secret,
And again we found ourselves in custody.

CHORUS
Sail etc

My husband and my baby
Died from fever at Batavia,
And monstrous Captain Edwards
Took away my liberty.
And the final devastation,
My little Charlotte died,
She was buried in my tears, and in the sea.

Newgate Prison was as dreadful
As the time when I had left it,
I'd sailed across the ocean
Consigned to Botany Bay,
But the kindly Mr. Boswell
Pleaded for me and they freed me.
I am Mary, the girl from Botany Bay.

CHORUS
Sail etc.

Benelong was befriended by Governor Phillip.
Engraving by S.J. Neele from La Trobe Picture Collection, State Library of Victoria

CHAPTER 6

Benelong & The White Sea Eagle

> "He was a thorough savage..."
>
> Sydney Gazette, 9 January 1813

In order to demonstrate that he was favourably disposed towards 'the Indians', Governor Phillip authorised the capture of three Aboriginal men. Arabanoo, the first man captured, quickly died from smallpox, an ominous sign of things to come. The second, Colby, 'slipped his hobbles' after a week. Benelong was held in custody for five months. During that time he was described variously as 'a bouncy, ebullient man, tender with children, something of a comedian, a bit of a rogue'. We do not know what he thought of his captors. Governor Phillip obviously liked Benelong.

Nonetheless, Benelong escaped in early 1790. No more was heard of him until September when he was recognised in a group of 200 men, one of whom threw a spear that wounded Governor Phillip. This was at a spot called Manly Cove, named thus by Phillip on an earlier visit when he met peacefully with a group of 'manly' Aboriginals. It did not take the Governor long to become disenchanted with the First Australians. He demanded 'heads in bags' after his personal huntsman, an unsavory character named McIntyre, was speared. But it seems that the Governor had a genuine affection for Benelong.

During his incarceration Benelong had developed a taste for rum, which was the currency of Port Jackson. After the arrival of the Second Fleet in 1791, Aboriginals began to gather in mendicant numbers on the outskirts of the penal colony. Benelong incurred the wrath of many of the new settlers who saw that he was pampered by Governor Phillip. A hut was erected for him at what is now called Benelong Point, the site of the magnificent Sydney Opera House.

In December 1792, at the end of his term as Governor, Phillip took Benelong with him to London. There he was dressed in the livery of the time and paraded as a 'noble savage'. His health deteriorated, but he was kept there for three years. In 1795 he returned to Australia on HMS *Reliance*.

He was to live until 3 January 1813, when he died aged about 50 years. An editorial comment in *The Sydney Gazette* of 9 January 1813 said:

> Bennelong (sic) died on Sunday morning last at Kissing Point. Of this veteran champion of the native tribe little favourable can be said. His voyage to, and benevolent treatment in Great Britain, produced no change whatever in his manner and inclinations, which were naturally barbarous and ferocious. The principal Officers of Government had for many years endeavoured, by the kindest of usage, to wean him from his original habits, and draw him into a relish for civilised life; but every effort was in vain exerted, and for the last few years he has been but little noticed. His propensity to drunkenness was inordinate; and when in that state he was insolent, menacing and overbearing. In fact he was a thorough savage, not to be warped from the form and character that nature gave him, by all the efforts that mankind could use.

It had not taken long for the new British settlers to work out and let it be known what they thought of the First Australians, and who they thought was in charge of the country.

Benelong & The White Sea Eagle

As I stood by Mrs Macquarie's Chair
In the knowledge that Benelong once stood there
A strange, chilling feeling came upon me
I seemed to hear a mournful song
The click of boomerangs as Benelong
Sang to his spirit, The White Sea Eagle

Ngananana   ngaiyu ga nara muruganga
Ngananana   ngaiyu ga nara murugnaga
Ngananana   ngaiyu ga nara muruganga
Ga   nara muruganga ngaiyu ngananana

There was an eerie sense of history on Yurong
It seemed haunted by the spirit of the man named Benelong
And I couldn't help thinking of that fateful day
The day that Governor Phillip came to stay
The day The White Sea Eagle flew away

The eagle flew up into the sky
It soared above the cliff tops high
Screeched down its message to Benelong
'Beware' was the warning call
But the people ran off, one and all
To watch the white man's ships as they sailed in

I couldn't help thinking that Benelong
Never again sang the eagle's song
For he seemed just like a man whose spirit left him
Doomed was he forever more
He lost his way as he lost his law
And The White Sea Eagle sings its song alone

Ngananana   ngaiayu ga nara muruganga etc.

Prisoners are rounded up; many bound for new and harsher regimes on Norfolk Island and Tasmania.
By permission of the Dixson Library, State Library of New South Wales

CHAPTER 7

No Worse, There Is None

> **Ne plus ultra, Norfolk Island
> No worse, there is none here on earth**
>
> **Ted Egan, *The Convicts***

In 1813, the year of Benelong's death, the Blue Mountains west of Sydney were crossed by explorers Gregory Blaxland, William Lawson and William Wentworth. It had taken 25 years to establish what lay inland. Typically, nobody had thought to ask the local Aboriginals if there were any traditional paths across the mountains. The appetites of the British were whetted by the prospect of taking up the huge fertile country now revealed. Schemes to attract free settlers were implemented. At the same time, new and tougher convict stations were established to handle the hardened criminals and in particular the recidivists. This was to dispel rumours circulating in Britain that emancipated convicts in Australia were being granted land and could anticipate a much better lifestyle than that prevailing for free people at home.

Norfolk Island and Van Diemen's Land (Tasmania) were to be the toughest stations. Norfolk Island had been occupied benignly by the British from 1788 to 1814. Soldiers and male and female convicts lived together harmoniously. They were self-sufficient. Then the island was abandoned and the convicts transferred to Tasmania. Less than ten years later, a decision was taken to re-establish Norfolk Island as the *ne plus ultra* of penal stations, the hell-on-earth that would be described in detail across Britain and Ireland, in the hope that the prospect of being sent there would deter criminals.

From 1829 until 1853, a succession of monstrous commandants was sent to Norfolk Island, a true Garden of

Eden in the Pacific Ocean. The official records of floggings are almost beyond belief. After all the flesh had been removed from their backs, convicts were flogged on their legs and on the soles of their feet. Fifteen hundred lashes were administered to five men - 300 lashes each - on one morning before the sun had risen. Convicts were tortured with devices like the Tube Gag: spread-eagled on a triangle and fitted with a bridle, the bit of which was a plug of ironwood with a small hole bored in the middle, prisoners broke their teeth as they sought to breathe. The determination of the commandants was matched only by the attitudes of the convicts, the 'hard men' who developed and fostered a brotherhood based on suicide pacts, stoicism and sodomy. Mutinies, murders and madness were the way of life. It is hard to appreciate today, in the tranquility of the tourist paradise that is Norfolk Island, that this was arguably the most evil place ever created on earth. The ghosts are laid, even at Murderers Mound, where the initiators of the 1834 Mutiny were unceremoniously buried in unhallowed ground.

Van Diemen's Land was established as a penal station in 1804 to handle the overflow from Port Jackson. Gradually, the name Tasmania came into use for Australia's island state. It was almost as tough as Norfolk Island as a convict settlement, but in later years life there was tempered by the increasing presence of free settlers. There are many stories of successful emancipists in Tasmania. But not all was tranquil. The cat of nine tails was in constant use. Hardened convicts were separated and sent to places like Sarah (Settlement) Island in Macquarie Harbour on the remote west coast. Entry to this magnificent harbour is through a treacherous, narrow channel only 70 metres wide, the narrowest harbour entrance in the world, with tides swirling in all directions. This entrance was subsequently called Hell's Gates by the convicts. The sheltered waters of the harbour, fed from the mighty Gordon River, measure twice the area of Sydney Harbour. Here the ancient Huon pine trees were felled, then milled in saw pits by convicts, spurred on by relentless floggings. Sarah Island was the setting for Marcus Clark's *For the Term of his Natural Life*.

Because of the difficulty of transporting the milled pine through Hell's Gates and around the island to Hobart,

Commandant James Butler had the ingenious idea of building ships on Sarah Island and sailing these through Hell's Gates. Huon Pine is perfect for shipbuilding: it is impervious to rot and all termites, and extremely flexible. The tiny 11-acre island was landscaped using only shovels and wheelbarrows, to prepare a shipbuilding yard and launching slips. Two convicts, Cole and Gray, made the first ships, then a free settler, David Hoy of Hobart, was asked to go to Sarah Island, train convicts and take charge of the shipbuilding. Between 1828 and 1833, ships of up to 220 tonnes displacement were constructed. It was the largest output of any shipyard in Australia, in an era when ships were the only form of transport.

Although the newly constructed ships provided the means, escape from Sarah Island was considered impossible. Discipline was formidable. Alexander Pearce, subsequently nicknamed 'the Cannibal', escaped twice and ate his mates in order to survive. He was eventually captured and executed in 1824. Matthew Brady, 'everybody's darlin', also escaped from Macquarie Harbour in 1824 and led the authorities a merry dance for two years. He was a classic Robin Hood, charming to all, and a source of infatuation for the ladies. The frustrated Governor George Arthur put a price on Brady's head, but the bushranger responded by offering a keg of rum to anybody prepared to deliver the Governor to him. Brady had no takers, and his luck ran out in 1826. Despite huge public support for a reprieve, Brady was hanged on 4 May that year, aged 27 years.

> You certainly were a bolter, Matthew Brady
> You certainly were a wild Colonial Lad
> Admired by all the chaps and loved by every lady
> You very nearly drove old Governor Arthur mad.
> Ted Egan, *Brady the Bolter*

After ten convicts stole the *Frederick*, a brig of 120 tonnes built at Sarah Island, Governor Arthur closed down the station and built a new 'hard prison' at Port Arthur, south east of Hobart.

Governor Arthur is a much-maligned figure in Tasmanian history. He is generally blamed for the genocide of the Tasmanian Aboriginals. For many years white people in

Australia believed that all Tasmanian Aboriginals were gone, and that Governor Arthur was responsible. Lurid tales about his 'Black War' found their way into school history texts. The truth is much more complicated. Although it is true that Governor Arthur sought to capture all Aboriginals on the island of Tasmania and accordingly drew a 'Black Line' on the map - his intention was to resettle them in areas exclusively reserved as Aboriginal land. The campaign failed, but the decimation of the Aboriginal population continued, as a result of hostilities, disease and many kidnappings of Aboriginal women by lawless men who hunted seals around the islands and along the southern coast of the Australian continent. It is true that there are no Tasmanian Aboriginals of full descent today, but there are many thousands of descendants of the First Tasmanians, proud of their inheritance and anxious to redress the wrongs of the past.

It is not widely known that Canadian and American convicts were also sent to the Australian penal colonies in 1840, after riots in Canada that sought to end British rule there. Some went to Norfolk Island, some to Tasmania. The story is told by Jack Cahill in his book, *Forgotten Patriots*.

> On 28 April 1996 horror returned to Port Arthur. A madman, Martin Bryant, rampaged around the ruins of the convict station with a carload of automatic firearms. He killed thirty-five people before he was captured. He was sentenced to life imprisonment, with no option of parole.
>
> As a result of Bryant's devastating onslaught, the Australian Government, led in forthright fashion by Prime Minister John Howard, effected a huge 'buy-back' of automatic firearms, and stringent gun laws were implemented.

*Paddy Uluru, custodian of the famous rock of the same name,
Uluru, 1975.*
Photo: Ted Egan

CHAPTER 8

The First Australians

> "You come my country, Tiwi Islands.
> Plenty fish, plenty song, plenty story."
>
> **Aloysius Puantulara (1987)**

Today in Australia the official definition of a First Australian is that he or she is "a person of Aboriginal or Torres Strait Islander descent, who claims to be such and is recognised as such by other Aboriginals and Torres Strait Islanders". The First Australians are today's descendants of the people who occupied Australia, both the mainland and the various islands including Tasmania, before 1788.

At the start of the 21st century, the First Australians, identified by themselves and on their terms in the National Census, numbered around 500,000. There is no way of knowing what their population numbers were in 1787, before the arrival of the British. Estimates range from 300,000 to 750,000. What is indisputable is that, when the First Fleet arrived, the entire continent of Australia was occupied by Aboriginal tribes or clans, speaking several hundred different languages. In some parts there were regional languages shared by several groups but, by and large, the languages had little in common. Today, about 40 survive and are used as a first language by about 30,000 people. But *all* of the traditional languages of Australia are under threat. Urgent action is needed to promote, preserve and encourage their continuing use, for they are some of the oldest languages in the world.

The Torres Strait Islanders are people of mixed Melanesian and Polynesian descent who live in the tiny islands of the Torres Strait, the waters separating Australia from Papua New Guinea. These people always lived, and still live in houses, in villages on their small islands. They harvest the ocean and grow crops; they are sedentary in lifestyle. Many have settled in mainland Australia

The Aboriginals, Caucasian people sometimes referred to as Australoids, have been in Australia for thousands of years - certainly in excess of 40,000 years - and they are arguably the longest established people on earth. Did they come here from Asia? Gondwanaland? Did life evolve in Australia? Who knows? They are certainly the First Australians, with a long-standing claim over this land.

In areas where traditional language is retained, children are still 'initiated'. Tiwi boys perform the 'shark dance'.

Photo: Allan Howard

In the cold southern regions of Australia, Aboriginals wore cloaks of marsupial skins.
Photo: Department of Aboriginal Affairs

There is an overriding similarity in the lifestyle adopted by the various First Australian Aboriginal groups. All were traditionally hunters and gatherers, none erected permanent buildings, no one saw the need to grow crops or domesticate animals. They were nomadic, walking the land and following the seasons to find Nature's harvests, but never wandering mindlessly - as some people believe and their critics assert. There are regional variations governed by the climate and the local environment. In the colder southern regions in earlier times, cloaks made of the skins of marsupial animals were worn in winter. In most parts of Australia, where there is a temperate climate, people went totally naked all of the time. In the desert areas of arid Central Australia, the Aboriginals were among the toughest people on earth, able to resist searing heat in the summer and freezing nights in the winter, always naked. They still live in the same country, still conscious of the traditional lifestyle. Nowadays they wear clothing, travel in motor cars and many live in houses. But thousands still retain the knowledge necessary to survive off the land, if that is required of them. Older people are determined that old hunting and gathering skills are retained. Wise people realise that this can only be achieved through retention of ceremonies and language.

Fortunately, in tribal regions like the Central Desert areas of Northern Territory, South Australia and Western Australia, in Arnhem Land and the Kimberley, every child is initiated according to age-old practice. Australian is their first language. Vital ceremonies are still performed and understood.

Aboriginals in rich areas like the Murray Basin and the coastal regions had little need to wander far in search of food. Consequently they were easy-going by nature, and much of their ceremonial life was based on 'playabout' dances - generically today called Corroborees. In the tough inland desert regions, where a family might be required to walk for days and then share a small lizard and a handful of water as their sustenance, there was no place for frivolity; there were inflexible attitudes and rigid rules about how to survive. Helpless old people knew they would be left behind if unable to walk. Sickly babies were killed.

Because in all cases the population was small, and required to stay small, stringent kinship rules were established to prevent inbreeding and promote social harmony. These ingenious laws persist to the present day among those First Australians who still speak their traditional languages and perform their age-old ceremonies. The crowned houses of Europe failed to recognise the need to establish similar conventions, and were plagued accordingly by the consequences of inbreeding.

It is a challenge not to talk in the past tense about Aboriginal life. There are many thousands of people whose first language is Australian, who still retain the knowledge, the songs and the ceremonies of their ancestors. Long may that continue and thrive.

The main purpose of Aboriginal life is to live in harmony with Nature. The land is of prime importance, for the ceremonies must be held at the right time and in the right place to ensure that nothing is left to chance. A person is born to an inheritance based on the prior and proper selection of its parents. He or she inherits inflexible kinship obligations and an ongoing commitment to understand how, when and where to get food.

Aboriginals do not accord any superior status to human beings. The land and *all* its creatures are one and inseparable. Any part in this total relationship is at risk if separated from other parts. The great ceremonies are increase rituals, which pay tribute to Nature in all its forms. Ceremonies for initiation, mourning and retribution are minor by comparison, but nonetheless important.

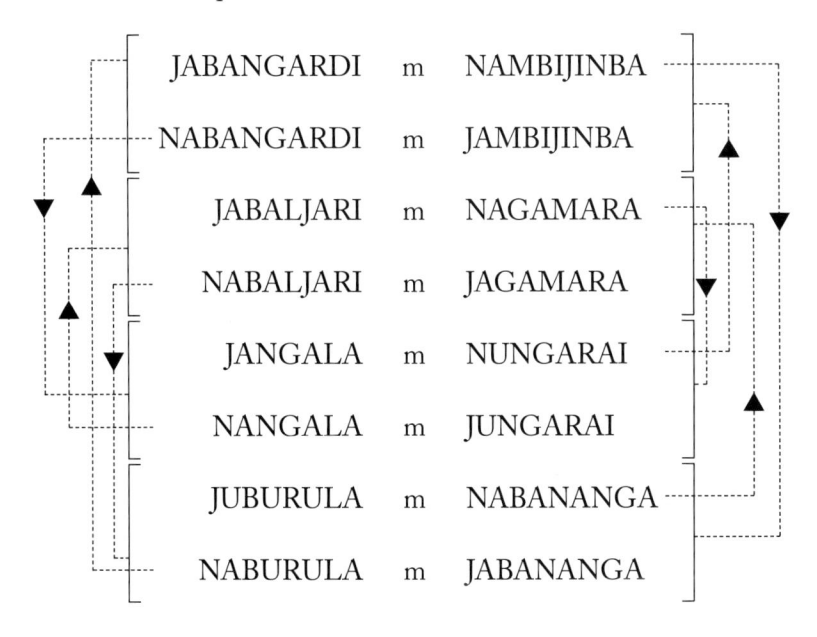

JABANGARDI	m	NAMBIJINBA
NABANGARDI	m	JAMBIJINBA
JABALJARI	m	NAGAMARA
NABALJARI	m	JAGAMARA
JANGALA	m	NUNGARAI
NANGALA	m	JUNGARAI
JUBURULA	m	NABANANGA
NABURULA	m	JABANANGA

The above diagram outlines the kinship rules of the Warlpiri tribe of Central Australia. Male group names begin with "J". Female group names begin with "N". Follow the arrows. A Jabangardi man marries a Nambijinba woman. The mother (not the father) determines the group of the children. Her sons are Jabananga. Her daughters are Nabananga. A Nabananga woman marries a Juburula man. Her sons are Jagamara. Her daughters are Nagamara. Keep following the arrows to see how the ongoing alliances occur through ensuing generations.

As Australia was 'taken up' by the new settlers, arbitrary lines were drawn on maps, totally ignoring the ongoing presence of Aboriginal people, and completely disdainful of their

Thousands of years of living off the land have made Aboriginals of the Australian desert some of the toughest people on earth.
Photo: Ted Egan

occupancy rights - dare one say, *ownership*. So certain was the British belief in the doctrine of *terra nullius*, that a blind spot was created in the psyche of non-Aboriginal Australians from the time of first contact.

To this day, the hardest thing to get into the Australian mindset is that the land was effectively stolen from the Aboriginals. Otherwise intelligent people will offer the wildest rationalisation to accommodate their own title to land, and thereby deny any possibility of a prior Aboriginal connection. This is exacerbated by the fact that very few Australians have ever studied Australian history in a real sense. Most never have any contact with Aboriginal people, for sadly their numbers have been reduced in direct proportion to the value of the land.

White, non-Aboriginal people in pretty country towns set on the banks of rivers, will declare: "there were no darkies here in the olden days. When my grandfather came here, it was virgin country". On marginal land, on the outskirts of the same towns, on the banks of the same (but now polluted) rivers, invariably live the despised remnants of the dispossessed First Australians. Not quite out of sight, but effectively out of mind. A seemingly intelligent white man remarked recently in Central Australia: "There were no coons around here until the white man put in the water bores". Another said: "There was no blackfellow interest in Uluru (Ayers Rock) until Bill Harney, a famous white bushman, told them it was important".

Near Cloncurry in northwest Queensland, a memorial was erected in 1988 to mark the bicentenary of British settlement in Australia, and to recognise the fact that the Kalkadoon people have lived in that region for countless centuries. It is not mentioned that the Kalkadoon suffered one of the biggest massacres in Australian history at the hands of the Queensland police. There is simply a message of peace and reconciliation. The monument was vandalised immediately. A bronze plaque of a warrior is riddled with high-velocity bullets. Sadly, such is the mindset of some people that, as soon as it is restored, it is desecrated again. Some intellectual 'giant' has scrawled across the monument: "It's our land too". At least the messages are becoming less provocative: earlier graffiti was more likely to say: "Kill all coons".

In recent years negative stories about Aboriginals have been constantly on the front pages of newspapers and on the airwaves. Many open minded people of all races are disenchanted with lurid stories of Aboriginal activists, so-called leaders, many of whom are self centred 'snouters', ripping-off public funds for themselves and their cronies while purporting to be working for the advancement of their race. It is easy to take a hardline stance and label their claims to be unreal or unreasonable. The great pity is that real injustices against Aboriginals are often put in the same category.

Mawalan Marika, original plaintiff in the Yirrkala land rights case, was told "the land owns the Aboriginals"
Photo: Ted Egan

CHAPTER 9

Land Rights: The Gentle Persuader

> Born to a destiny, gentle persuader
> Simple demands, nothing more, nothing less
> Take on the Government
> Take on Lord Vestey
> Battles to fight, finally success.
>
> Ted Egan, *Old Vincent*

In 1966 an elderly, dignified Aboriginal stockman named Vincent Lingiari caused the words 'land rights' to be introduced for the first time into the Australian vernacular. Sporadic claims about dispossession, made by small Aboriginal groups of protesters in the southern capitals of Melbourne and Sydney in the 1930s were largely ignored or ridiculed. This was different: Lingiari's timing was fortunate. There was the medium of television that could take his fascinating, straightforward, eminently reasonable claims to the rest of Australia, indeed the world. It is an archetypal *David* v. *Goliath* story. Here was an illiterate, penniless, seemingly powerless Aboriginal, acknowledged as a wonderful stockman after a lifetime working for white bosses in the Australian cattle industry. He had taken on the combined forces of Lord Vestey, cattle baron of England, and Vestey's real estate agent, the Australian Federal Government.

For a pittance, the Australian Government had leased to Vestey the huge Wave Hill cattle station, on the basis that its 5,000 square miles was Crown Land. The station was located in the remote northwest of the Northern Territory, on land traditionally occupied by the Gurindji tribe. Many of the

Gurindji people had been shot by early white settlers. The remainder had worked for various lessees on Wave Hill Station from the 1880s. In 1953, after 70 years of loyal and very tough work, the Gurindji stockmen were given their first touch of the white man's money. At the Wave Hill Races each Aboriginal worker was given a £5 note to spend.

On strike: Pincher Numiari, head stockman for the Gurindji cattle station, 1975
Photo: Ted Egan

Lingiari had been head stockman of one of the Wave Hill stock camps for many years. His people worked in serf-like conditions from dawn to dark, as the labour force overseeing 80,000 cattle. In 1966, Lingiari led his people as they 'walked off' the station. His protest was simple: he was "tired of being treated worse than a dog". When interviewed, he went on to say: "I got stories from my old Grandpa that this land belonging to me before the horse and the cattle came over". When news of the walk-out reached Darwin, capital of the Northern Territory, government officials scoffed and said: "The Gurindji will be starved back into submission in a week".

A senior Federal Government minister was blunt: "If these Gurindji people want to get some land, why don't they do what any other decent Australian would do? Why don't they save their money and buy some land?" (Sorry, minister, you were not present at the Wave Hill races in 1953.) Lingiari's resolve hardened. He took his case to sympathetic trade union leaders in Darwin and interstate. His cause was supported by unionists and university students. Enough money was raised to enable him to head a seven year strike, the longest in Australian history.

The Australian government did nothing. Quick to realise the political ramifications of the dispute, Lord Vestey asked Colonel Patrick Montgomerie of the Anti-Slavery Society in London to visit Australia in 1970. Montgomerie travelled to Wave Hill and immediately recommended that the Vestey organisation should offer to surrender half the Wave Hill lease, including cattle, to the Gurindji Aboriginals. That offer was made by Lord Vestey, but the Prime Minister at the time, William McMahon, refused to transfer the land. It was Crown Land, not Aboriginal land, he said.

There were huge demonstrations by students, unions and other supporters. A young woman was carrying a banner at one of these marches demanding LAND RIGHTS FOR THE GURINDJI. A tough bystander said to her: "You wouldn't know the difference between a Gurindji and a barramundi." The student replied: "And I don't care, as long as they both get their land rights."

A Labor Federal Government was elected in Australia in 1972. One of its principal platforms was that justice in land matters would be accorded to Aboriginals. The new Prime Minister, Gough Whitlam, moved quickly to effect the transfer of a 2,500 square mile lease to the Gurindji people at Wave Hill. The following year Whitlam went to Wave Hill to hand over the lease.

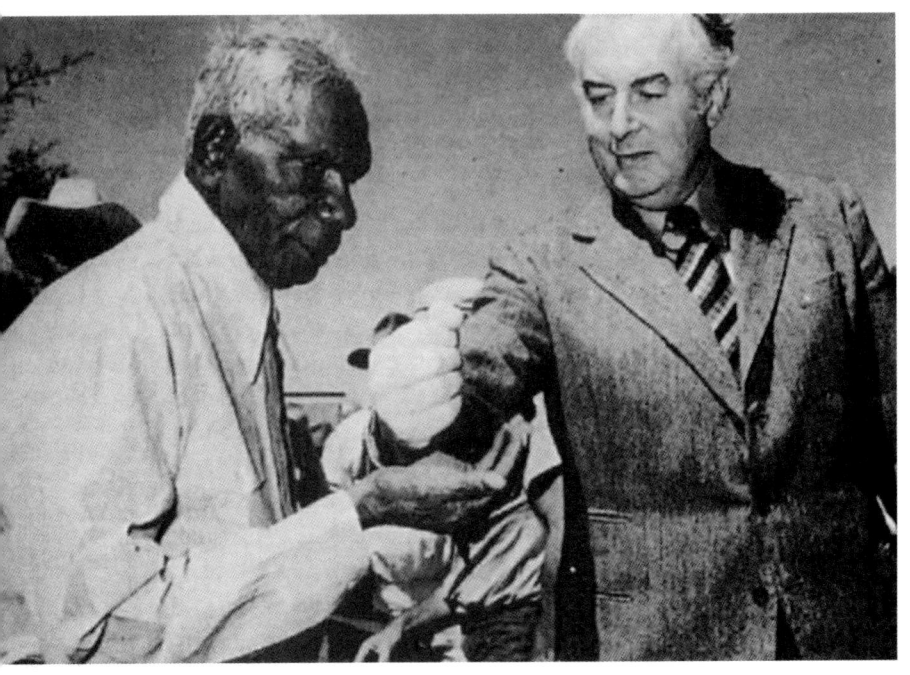

Symbolic gesture: Prime Minister Gough Whitlam pours soil into the welcoming hand of Vincent Lingiari at Wave Hill, 1975
Photo: Merv Bishop

The real matter of justice in land had not yet been addressed, however. Wave Hill was still Crown Land. But in 1969 a group of three Aboriginal clan leaders challenged the entire British system of land tenure.

In 1963 a mining lease had been given to a foreign company to explore the mineral potential of north east Arnhem Land, in the Northern Territory. It was established that there were huge deposits of bauxite, the mineral used to produce aluminium, on land that white people began to call the Gove Peninsula. Peter Gove was a RAAF pilot killed in the region during World War II. A Methodist mission station had been established in 1935 with Aboriginal consent at a place called Yirrkala, on the same peninsula. When the lease was awarded, the Methodist missionaries, particularly the Reverend Edgar Wells, assisted and encouraged the Aboriginal people to petition the Federal Government. A short letter written in both English and *Gupapuyngu*, the traditional Australian language of the region, was signed by three clan elders. At the same time they presented a huge painting using earth ochres on eucalyptus bark, which told the story of their Dreamtime ancestors who had bestowed the land irrevocably to today's claimants. The Bark Petition still hangs in Australia's national capital, Canberra. But it raised little other than mirth in Parliament in 1963. Yes, a Parliamentary inquiry was established, and created a lot of tut-tutting, but in 1969 the claims of Aboriginals were totally ignored when the entire Gove Peninsula was leased to Nabalco, a consortium of Australian and Swiss companies, for the extraction of bauxite. The mining would effectively lower over 800 square miles of landscape by twenty metres. Royalties would be paid into a fund to be administered by a board for the benefit of *all* Aboriginal people in the Northern Territory, not directly to the Aboriginal owners.

  The Aboriginals took their cause to the Supreme Court of the Northern Territory. The case became known as *Milirrpum v. Nabalco and the Commonwealth of Australia.* After six months of hearings at Yirrkala and Darwin Judge Blackburn handed down his verdict. He denied the Aboriginal claims to ownership of the land. It was, in fact, quite a learned judgment, but it was constructed by the Judge under the principles of the same British system that, he *held*, now superseded and overruled any prior authority in the land. One of Blackburn's more memorable utterances, often quoted, was that, under their system, "the Aboriginals do not own the land: the land owns the Aboriginals".

  The Yirrkala Aboriginals were devastated. Bauxite mining commenced. Later on things would change for the better.

  Obiter dictum, Judge Blackburn recommended that action be taken to allow the intrinsic needs of Aboriginals in similar cases to be assisted, through the implementation of new land regulations. The Whitlam Government set up a Royal

Commission in 1973, the Woodward Land Rights inquiry, headed by Justice Woodward, previously counsel for the Yirrkala Aboriginals. His Commission produced enlightened recommendations that were slowly implemented, creating a system allowing land title to be granted to Aboriginal groups where it was established that they retained language and customs that were in place prior to the coming of white settlers.

An important proviso was that there be no conflict with any other form of legal land title held by anybody else. It was relatively easy for the immediate transfer of Land title to groups who lived on Aboriginal Reserves where there was no other conflicting tenure. In the case of the Yirrkala Aboriginals, the mining leases to Nabalco were not withdrawn, but the Aboriginals were granted direct payment of royalties and granted Native Title over the remainder of their country. Sacred sites on the Gove Peninsula were identified and protected, but not before the occurrence of minor desecration by bulldozers near the new township of Nhulunbuy.

About one-third of the total land area of the Northern Territory was immediately granted to Aboriginal groups on an irrevocable basis.

At the outset the new form of Aboriginal Title could apply only to those areas of Australia where federal law claimed precedence over state law. The basic principle of the Australian Commonwealth constitution is that the defined, established rights of the six founding states (New South Wales, Queensland, Victoria, South Australia, Tasmania and Western Australia) at the time of Federation in 1901 are prescribed and enshrined, and all other rights are the province of the Federal Government. This meant that the findings of the Woodward Royal Commission were capable of being implemented in 1975 in the Northern Territory, where there were about 30,000 Aboriginals with traditional claims - and ongoing connections with their land - and the Australian Capital Territory, where there are very few First Australians with traditional connections.

The only state willing to relinquish land to Aboriginals on traditional grounds was South Australia. The governments of Western Australia, Queensland, and subsequently the Northern Territory, with comparatively large numbers of Aboriginals and

Torres Strait Islander populations, mounted bitter legal and regulatory defences every time a land claim was made on behalf of any Aboriginal group.

Then came *Mabo*, a four letter word that will have Australia in a state of litigation, division and turmoil over land for at least the next 500 years.

Eddy Mabo was a Torres Strait Islander from a very remote island named Mer, otherwise known as Murray Island. He was an activist in all matters, especially those concerning land ownership. He had been banished from his island to the Australian mainland by a particularly sinister Queensland state government which branded him a trouble maker. Mabo eventually mounted a case to claim that he had recognisable and established land rights on Murray Island that dated back beyond any foreign occupation of Australia. After a bitter, ten-year passage through the lower courts, Mabo's case eventually reached the High Court, the final arbiter in Australian law. Mabo died while the High Court was hearing the case. Such was the bitterness, that his family had to re-bury his remains privately when his original grave was constantly desecrated. But Mabo's death was not the end of the case. Murray Island elders became the plaintiffs and the High Court ruled in their favour. There was no further appeal possible.

In essence, the Court found that the doctrine of *terra nullius* should never have been applied at the time of British settlement, but that British sovereignty was nonetheless legal and therefore all freehold title was valid. However, where it could be established that there was unbroken connection between Aboriginal groups and their land, in terms of language, land usage and ceremonial life, as was clearly the case with Mabo, the land ownership of that group could be established and recognised Australia wide as Aboriginal Title. Aboriginal Land Councils established after the Woodward Commission quickly lodged claims for most of the unalienated Crown Land in Australia.

Conservative political bodies in the Australian states went berserk. Election campaigns featured advertisements showing black hands slowly grabbing the land. Householders were encouraged to believe that 'it will be your house in the suburbs that they will take next'. Hard-nosed attitudes became the order of the day.

In 1996 there was another High Court decision, which has become known simply as 'Wik'. (The prefix 'wik' is applied to Aboriginal language groups in north Queensland, for example, wik-Munkan.) In the 'Wik' case a group of Aboriginal plaintiffs sought to establish traditional rights over land they insisted was theirs but which had been denied them by leases the government had created on the Cape York Peninsula. The High Court ruled in their favour. The Federal Liberal government immediately responded with a Ten Point Plan to weaken the Aboriginal position; this led to confusion. The paradox was that Prime Minister John Howard defended his government's divisive actions as 'promoting national unity'! Rhetoric ruled: facts were forgotten. It was quickly established that there were no positive votes in a pro-Aboriginal stance. Aboriginal groups and their supporters became more vehement in their demands. But they were electorally powerless; two percent of the population, too few altogether.

It is fortunate that among state governments there is today a commendable, positive attitude to land matters and Aboriginal ownership. In the Northern Territory, the Labor Government now negotiates with established traditional owners when land is needed for housing, mining or other developmental purposes. This policy seems to be working. It is often as easy as calling it Aboriginal land instead of Crown land.

But generally, attitudes in Aboriginal matters are now polemicised to an almost impossible level and it is hard to establish the truth. Even if a very reasonable Aboriginal claim is made, many instinctively see it as economic blackmail. Sometimes that is true. Aboriginals traditionally had to be strong and resolute. They had to obey Nature's rules to survive in this harsh land. Sadly, in today's Australia, Aboriginals are not required to use those same skills and beliefs any more. Particularly in rural and tribal regions, where deprivation and demoralisation are very real factors, they are marginalised to a point where they are unemployable, apart from menial jobs created around their own needs. And yet government funding is at a level where the simplest of jobs in Aboriginal Affairs are given to white people, often of questionable ability. The unfortunate First Australians seem doomed to be forever on the welfare treadmill and most other people, regrettably, see that as the only option. Where Nature once provided, now the Government takes over. There must be taxpayer funding for every Aboriginal need, and every need is labelled 'a problem'.

Unfortunately, governments do not help. Instead of looking for real solutions to the many injustices that still prevail, it is easy for guilt-stricken, devious, ignorant or 'bleeding-hearts' politicians to shovel heaps of taxpayers' money at so-called problems and claim: "We are determined to resolve this. Look how much money we are spending". If only money truly solved problems. The sinister aspect to all of this mix-up is that so many schemes and solutions proposed for, or foisted upon, Aboriginal groups are doomed to failure, and are a waste of taxpayers' money. The role of government is to ensure that problems continue to be problems. People opposed to Aboriginal causes and interests can then point the finger of scorn with impunity. It becomes disarmingly easy to dismiss authentic claims. "Justice in land: you've got to be joking. We've paid for the country ten times over", say the hard-heads.

The cruel, inescapable fact is that in Australia at the start of the 21st century the First Australians are the poorest, worst-housed, least-educated, least employed, most unhealthy, most demoralised, most incarcerated, worst victims of alcohol and substance abuse, of all identifiable groups of people in this otherwise affluent, fortunate land. Their critics say: "We give them all that money, and they piss it up against the wall." Aboriginals respond: "You took our land and our culture away from us. We didn't invite you and your greedy system to our country. Don't expect us to be reasonable. It's all your fault."

Neither attitude is of any consequence. Dynamic leadership must be encouraged, and despite fanciful rhetoric about self-management of their destiny by Aboriginals, it is obvious that Aboriginal leaders must be able, and prepared, to draw on the entire resources of the nation, including the skills of non-Aboriginals where necessary. They cannot 'go it alone': we have been taking their decision-making processes away from them for 200 years, and they are not suddenly going to manifest business and planning skills just because we have given up on them in real terms and handed them a cheque book as 'conscience-money'.

And it is just not economic change that is required. Aboriginal society is shattered to such an awful level that the total social skill of the nation, properly and compassionately applied, must be brought to bear in areas like physical and mental health, domestic violence, child abuse and low life expectancy. A body like ATSIC (Aboriginal and Torres Strait Islands Commission) must continue to be elected democratically from the Roll of First Australians, and must be empowered to take the required initiatives to effect real solutions to problems. ATSIC must be funded on a predictable and responsible level, as of right, not as charity.

It will not be easy. It does not alter their right to an identity as Aboriginals or Torres Strait Islanders, but an overwhelming majority of contemporary First Australians are not of the full descent. Their critics say: "If they keep marrying whites, as most seem to, are they still Aboriginals?" Some look so un-Aboriginal they tend to invite some level of discrimination or friction to prove themselves. They live a total western existence, have no Australian language, and no real knowledge or adherence to traditional practices or lifestyle. That only exacerbates their losses and problems in the minds of many First Australians.

There is a determined effort among them to regenerate traditional culture and that is commendable, if sometimes spurious. Pale-skinned people play didgeridoos, a practice once common only to the northern coastal regions of Australia, and perform 'ceremonies'. That sometimes attracts ridicule and rancour from their critics but it is nonetheless a display of pride, previously denied them, in the lifestyle and belief system shattered by the institutionalism forced upon them. It is hardly 'traditional culture', but it unites them under their flag of red, black and gold. As one Aboriginal woman fiercely admonished a critic (the author!): "We'll do our dances any way we like, and if we want to, we'll wear pink chiffon".

Time is on their side. Fortunately all the old discriminatory 'whitefeller' laws were repealed long ago. It is nowadays a badge of honour to have Aboriginal blood in one's veins. And it is

The call for land rights became a chorus amongst the Aboriginals towards the end of the 20th century. Aboriginal women demand their rights in Alice Springs, 1981
Photo: Carmel Sears

some consolation that in three important areas - sport, music, and the arts - Aboriginals are more than equals. It is incumbent upon all Australians that Aboriginals be encouraged in those areas. But at the same time, meaningful strategies must be put in place to provide opportunities in all walks of life. After all, they are the First Australians.

Gurindji Blues

Poor bugger me, Gurindji
Me bin sit down this country
Long time before the Lord Vestey
Allabout land belongin' to we
Oh poor bugger me, Gurindji.
Poor bugger blackfella, Gurindji
Long time work no wages we
Work for the good old Lord Vestey
Little bit flour, sugar and tea
For the Gurindji, from Lord Vestey,
Oh poor bugger me.

Poor bugger me, Gurindji
Man called Vincent Lingiari
Talk long allabout Gurindji
"Daguragu place for we,
Home for we, Gurindji."
But poor bugger blackfella, Gurindji,
Government boss him talk long we
"Build you house with electricity,
But at Wave Hill, for can't you see,
Wattie Creek belong to Lord Vestey?"
Oh, poor bugger me.

Poor bugger me, Gurindji,
Up come Mr Frank Hardy
ABSCHOL * too, and talk long we
Givit hand long Gurindji
Buildim house and plantim tree
Longa Wattie Creek for Gurindji.
But poor bugger blackfella, Gurindji
Government law him talk long we
Can't givit land long blackfella, see,
Only spoilim Gurindji
Oh poor bugger me.

Poor bugger me, Gurindji,
Peter Nixon talk long we:
"Buy you own land, Gurindji,
Buyim back from the Lord Vestey,"
Oh poor bugger me, Gurindji.
Poor bugger blackfella, Gurindji,
Suppose we buyim back country
What you reckon proper fee?
Might be flour, sugar and tea
From the Gurindji to Lord Vestey?
Oh poor bugger me.

Ngaiyu luyurr ngura-u
Sorry my country, Gurindji.

*ABSCHOL: A University Students Union group, promoting better schooling for Aboriginal people.

Today's 'Brown Skin Babies' are adopted by Aboriginal families.
Musso Harvey and his adopted son Archie.
Photo: Allan Howard

CHAPTER 10

The Stolen Generation

> From white man, boss, the baby I got
> Why he lettim take baby away?
>
> Bob Randall, *Brown Skin Baby*

Australia has a history of cruelty to children. Not so much the action of paedophiles, though there have been unhappy examples. More often than not, cruelty has been institutionalized by the separation of children from their families in the name of Christianity. Sometimes it was done on the grounds that the children would be better off and likely to get a more Christian upbringing if they were institutionalized rather than allowed to remain with their mothers and fathers.

It is doubtful whether Jesus would have approved of some of the things that have been carried out in his name. There is in Australia an official separation of Church and State but politics has always been dominated by religious axe-grinders seeking to impose their beliefs and standards on everybody else. Just as it was easy to rationalise the dreadful convict system, it was logical that a high level of institutionalism would enable the State and Churches to combine to remove children, particularly Aboriginals, considered to be 'at risk'.

'Put them in a Home'. Give them the disciplined upbringing that their 'stupid' parents should have had the good sense to impose. Poor, neglected and under-privileged children are part of 'God's burden'. They are the means whereby rich, privileged, powerful people can earn that elusive 'after life'. And, as if there were not enough local children to worry about, the Australian government combined with British authorities to bring thousands of children from Britain to institutions in Australia.

In 1932 there were 50,000 children in various institutions around Australia: orphanages, foundling homes, foster homes, homes for wayward girls, homes for unmarried mothers, detention centres, and prisons for junior offenders. Most of these places were run by religious organisations. *Discipline* was the operative word: if Jesus Christ was running the show it would have been *Love*. Suffer the little children.

Today, the midnight-to-dawn radio talk back shows are dominated by people (why aren't they sleeping peacefully?) telling of the horror of their incarceration in those institutions. The thrashings, the deprivation, the horrendous sexual abuse at the hands of their so-called Christian benefactors, the ongoing nightmares, psychiatric problems, the bed-wetting, and perhaps worst of all, the 'inability to touch or be touched'. They cannot all be lying, or fabricating these stories. The saddest message that comes through all of these attempts to 'unburden the load' is that the narrators, reared without love and the benefit of normal family life, are so often unable themselves to have normal relationships or raise happy families.

In the 1990s this emerged as a very emotive Aboriginal issue. Defined as 'the stolen generations', it came to be fiercely debated across the country. Once again, the real facts were ignored, distorted, and sadly, rejected by a large majority on the grounds that "if you give them (Aboriginals) an inch they'll take a mile". It is a very complex issue, but capable of some kind of honourable resolution, if only there was real national leadership based on decent human values and compassion.

It was easy to believe, at the time of Federation in 1901, that the First Australians would eventually disappear, and then there would be no further need to feel guilty about their dispossession. The new Australian Constitution contained a section ordaining that "in assessing the total population of the nation, aboriginal natives shall not be counted". Effectively, Aboriginals were deemed to be non-persons. (Subsequent South African governments closely studied Australia's tactics when, many years later, they created the sinister system of *apartheid*.) The numbers of First Australians had been drastically reduced by introduced diseases, massacres and conflict - with the spear eventually outmatched by the horse and the gun. In 1901 it was held that in Tasmania, there were no Aboriginals left. In Victoria, New South Wales and South Australia, where white settlement was the most concentrated, Aboriginals who survived were herded onto reserves and missions, out of sight and powerless. Frontier areas were gradually being *cleared* or *settled* - these are words that have always had sinister and sad connotations in Australia. The better land in all the states had been taken up by the time of Federation, and Aboriginals were no longer a legacy, burden or even an embarrassment for the 'pioneers' in those regions. The 'darkies' were 'on the way out'. 'Smooth the dying pillow' was the best advice proffered.

In the absence of many white women in frontier regions, embarrassing numbers of mixed-race children were being born. They were almost exclusively the result of unions between white men and black women (for the opposite union was considered inconceivable) and invariably based on the exploitation of the black women concerned.

A policy of 'assimilation' was proposed, whereby reserves for tribal Aboriginals would be created, places where they could safely but inevitably die out as a race. At the same time it was decreed that children of mixed-race should be taken from their families and placed in institutions where they could be trained in hygiene and work skills to be 'like white people'. Girls would be prepared for domestic service, boys for stock work and the trades. Marriage between the 'brown-skin babies' was not to be encouraged, but it was felt that girls with sufficient training might make good wives for some white men, usually in rural situations.

Nobody ever presented a policy statement concerning mixed-race boys. "Maybe if we don't discuss them they'll have the good sense to just disappear", it was said. In their enthusiasm for assimilation, authorities based their arguments on anthropology: Australia's Aboriginals, being Caucasian, did not 'throw back' in skin-colour terms. Cruder advocates of eliminating the Aboriginals as a race through miscegenation, called it 'fucking them white'.

It is not known precisely how many children were removed from their parents, but it is certain that they numbered in the thousands, over a period of around 100 years. It was a fortunate policy for the fathers of the children, who were often police, clergymen, politicians and other 'eminent pioneers'. It was convenient for their embarrassingly obvious coloured progeny to be taken out of their districts. In the early days, the removal was often effected forcibly, and sometimes violently, by the police. There are genuine reports of parents swimming rivers to hide from police sent to capture 'half castes' or 'yeller fellers' as they were sometimes called. Mothers often painted their fair skinned children with charcoal to pretend they were 'full-bloods'. It is important to stress in this matter that there was never any policy to remove children of the full descent in Aboriginal terms, the so-called full bloods. Laws were framed in the different states to classify children according to their breakdown in genetic inheritance - words like quadroon, octaroon, quarter-caste, half-caste, three-quarter-caste, even one-eighth, one-sixteenth, one-thirty-second caste, yes, one-sixty-fourth caste, were used advisedly. Children were sought for removal to different institutions not on the basis of their Aboriginality, but on their degree of whiteness. The Aboriginal content condemned them, the degree of whiteness determined their assimilation prospects. The film *Rabbit Proof Fence* shows Mr Neville, the Chief Protector of Aboriginals, running a practised eye over the children to determine who was 'white enough' for a particular institution. Again, the framers of South Africa's *apartheid* system were able to base their discerning colour laws on Australian writings about hair structure, nipple colour, and shades of pigmentation on strategic parts of the body. It was so scientific.

Particularly in latter years, it became the practice for authorities, in many cases through sincere, highly motivated people, to convince Aboriginal families that it was for the best that the mixed-race children receive training and education. It was relatively easy to get a type of consensus, for Aboriginals knew from experience who won in such situations. White authorities were so powerful, it was better to say "yes" and accommodate them. On mission stations, the white authorities had power of life and death over the Aboriginal inhabitants. The key of the ration store gave them that power.

As with most matters concerning the First Australians, it is hard to have rational argument in Australia about the stolen children. On one hand there is emotional talk, occasionally true, about 'being dragged from my mother's breast'. On the other hand people point to Aboriginals of mixed descent, who have acquired considerable skills in the prevalent western lifestyle, and ask: 'Aren't they better off than the bush blackfellows, now that we gave them such opportunities?' Some (few) Aboriginals of mixed-race say: 'To be taken away was the best thing that ever happened to me'. Many more deplore the separation from their families, their culture, their language, and entire meaning in life. Poignant and very true tales are told to this day of reunions of previously unknown brothers and sisters, or far-off families, sometimes after separation for fifty years or more. The saddest tales are those where there is now no common ground. 'I met my mother, but we had no level of communication. She was a stranger'.

It was all wrong, very wrong.

The official practice of 'removing' mixed-race children ceased throughout Australia by the 1960s, but there was thereafter widespread encouragement of single Aboriginal mothers of mixed-race children to give up their babies for adoption to the many childless white couples who wished to adopt 'a lovely little brown baby'. It became something of an industry. Sadly, the aftermath of many such adoptions was that things seemed to go well in early childhood, but then older children became traumatised after being called 'nigger' or somesuch at exclusive 'white' schools. "Who am I? What am I?" asks Bob Randall in his magnificent, searing song, *Brown Skin Baby*:

> Waradju, Waradju
> Tjitji abakatja ngaiyu puya kardingu
> Sorry, sorry,
> My brown-skinned baby, they take him away

After a Royal Commission in Australia investigated the inordinate number of 'deaths in custody' of so-called 'indigenous' people, it was *held* that one of the reasons for the high rates of imprisonment and the deplorable incidence of suicide, was their institutionalisation. Again it seemed that people raised in institutions had no benign experience to draw when they became parents. It was *held* also that psychological scarring had occurred to a shocking level, and that various steps should be taken within Australia to seek to heal the wounds. A report, called *Bringing Them Home* was compiled by former High Court Justice Sir Ron Wilson and Dr Mick Dodson, an eminent Aboriginal scholar, sportsman and activist.

Dr. Mick Dodson: his report urged Australians to say "Sorry".
Copyright: Terry Milligan. By permission of the National Library of Australia

Bringing Them Home asked the people of Australia to express their sorrow that there had ever been a policy in Australia to remove children from their families. The vast majority of Australians found it easy to offer such condolence, and many thousands signed 'Sorry Books' to that effect. Most State and Territory Parliaments passed 'Motions of Apology'.

Many populist radio 'shock-jocks' and similar-minded journalists ridiculed the report and its aftermath. The Federal Government, principally through Prime Minister Howard, strenuously and consistently refused to offer an official apology. His hard-headed advisors had obviously told the Prime Minister: "If you apologise to them, John, they'll immediately produce the invoice book". The problem was that, in the *absence* of an official apology, the litigation - and, yes, obviously with a view to compensation - commenced via several heart-breaking court cases about things like "fiduciary care', all of which were lost by the Aboriginal plaintiffs. Hurt people were now hard and shattered people.

The Report coincided with the 1994 formation of a Reconciliation Council comprised of prominent people; its membership had a majority of First Australians. It was a worthwhile exercise. The Council impressed the converted, those looking for 'a fair go' for Aboriginals and a unified society. Noble sentiments were expressed by a huge majority of black and white Australians. There were symbolic walks across bridges in capital cities; about 500,000 people walked across Sydney Harbour bridge. But the Council had little political impact. The Federal Government scoffed at notions of a treaty or any form of document that proclaimed prior ownership, even occupancy, of the continent by First Australians. And the bigots had their prejudices reinforced.

A simple solution would have been easy. A principled Prime Minister could have made a statement that went something like this: "I am deeply sorry that in our country, Australia, there were ever discriminatory laws based on race. Laws that separate people from their families, and especially where this concerns children, are morally wrong, and indefensible. There can be no question of monetary compensation in matters like this, for all such laws have long since been repealed. But as leader of our nation I offer an unreserved apology to any person or family affected by such laws, and I promise that similar discriminatory legislation or action will never be contemplated again in Australia."

David Marr provides an interesting appraisal of 'white, Christian' Australia, especially its political movers and shakers, in his book *The High Price of Heaven*. He asserts that, in Aboriginal matters, John Howard has the unequivocal belief that 'our obligation to black Australia (is) decent Christian charity. Their obligation to us (is) gratitude'.

It is a straightforward question of establishing right from wrong, and enabling the restoration of dignity. Amongst the first things we teach our children is 'let's say sorry, and start again'. But it seems there must always be a political agenda. This has been the case in all matters concerning Aboriginals since the arrival of Governor Phillip. The beads, mirrors and blankets were not straight-out gifts. They were the symbol that dispossession had begun.

Professor Lowitja O'Donoghue AM, MBE, Australian of the Year 1984, member of the stolen generation: reunited with her mother at age 30.
Photo: Ted Egan

There is a need to review all that has happened since that time, and perhaps start again, wherever possible. Goodwill and compassion are required ingredients. Twenty million Australians now share a safe, wonderfully endowed island continent that has been occupied by the First Australians as 'stewards' for countless thousands of generations. There has been a recent period of white occupancy, a mere 200 plus years, during which attempts have been made to 'conquer' the country rather than cherish and relate to it. It is not too late to change direction. But further delay will be tragic.

Brown Skin Baby

A young stockman used to ride
A quiet pony round the countryside
In a native camp, he'd never forget
A young black mother, her cheeks all wet

Yawi, Yawi, my brown skin baby
They takim away.

Between her sobs he heard her say:
"Police bin takim my baby away,
From white man, boss, the baby I got
Why he let him take baby away?"

Yawi, Yawi, my brown skin baby
They takim away.

On a mission station, far away,
The boy grew up, with a new name
For his mother he searched in vain
Upon this earth they never met again.

Yawi, Yawi, my brown skin baby
They takim away.

Ngundinadju pulkana ngura nanagarr
Kaiya pitjala kardingu
Ngura parari mulaba
Tjtiji abakadja ngaiyu puya kardingu

Waradju, waradju
Tjitji abakadja ngaiyu puya kardingu.

Caroline Chisholm: she called the women she brought to Australia 'God's Police'.
Portrait by A.C. Hayter

CHAPTER 11

Free Settlers: God's Police

> **You will never ever see your home again**
> **You will travel to Australia**
> **To a land of lawless men**
> **The weather and the work**
> **Will make you old before your time**
> **And you'll never, ever, see your home again**
>
> **Ted Egan, *God's Police***

The governorship of Lachlan Macquarie between 1809 and 1821 coincided with a period when many people began to think of Australia as their home rather than Britain. Emancipated convicts, refused re-entry to their native land, were encouraged to take up small plots. Better land became available as explorers pushed into more fertile country to the west and south of Sydney. Free settlers from Britain were encouraged. Many of those who came were relatively rich and influential. Governor Macquarie travelled extensively, even to Van Diemen's Land, and almost every significant natural feature was given a new name - Port Macquarie, Lake Macquarie, Macquarie River, Governor's Hill, and Lachlan River.

Convicts who had served their time were always called Emancipists. Former soldiers of the New South Wales Corps, prepared to stay in Australia, plus a small influx of free settlers, laid claim to as much land as they felt they needed. They were known as Exclusives. The Exclusives were able to use as much convict labour as they wished, and rich farms were quickly established. The notorious John Macarthur, who had led the 'Rum Rebellion' that saw the removal from office of Governor

Bligh, took up thousands of acres of land at Camden, near Sydney. He and, more particularly, his wife Elizabeth laid the foundations for the merino sheep herds that would eventually allow Australia to prosper from wool - 'the golden fleece' it was soon to be called.

There were around 50 males to one female in the population of the new colony, and all women were spoken for. It was realised that single women were needed to be attracted to Australia, and free passages were offered from Britain. At first this was carried out in a most haphazard way. Upon arrival in the ports of New South Wales and Van Diemen's Land, the supposedly free women were literally dragged off the ships and taken by the biggest or toughest men into conditions and destinies often worse than the lifestyles of convict women.

John Dunmore Lang: He wanted Australians to marry Scottish Presbyterian girls
By permission of La Trobe Picture Collection, State Library of Victoria

Two formidable figures emerged into the Australian political arena. John Dunmore Lang, who arrived in 1822, was a humourless, forthright, hell-and-damnation, anti-Papist, Presbyterian minister. Caroline Chisholm, who arrived six years later, was the beautiful, assertive Roman Catholic wife of an army officer transferred to Sydney from India. Chisholm and Lang were appalled at the treatment of not just the convicts but women in general. Each, in their own way, was determined to lobby the local authorities and the British Government for funding, and other forms of assistance, to allow them to bring migrants, especially large, supervised parties of single girls.

The two had their differences. Lang berated Chisholm's efforts on straight sectarian grounds. He sought to introduce Scottish, Protestant girls. Mrs Chisholm concentrated mainly on Ireland, and almost exclusively recruited Catholics, but she had a commendable track record of assisting all people in need regardless of race, colour or creed. In setting up her Homes for Women in Sydney and country centres in New South Wales, Mrs Chisholm's undeniable success earned her the begrudging support of Governor Gipps and other influential officials in London.

FREE FEMALE EMIGRATION posters went up all over Britain and Ireland, as subsequent Governors of New South Wales and Tasmania joined Lang and Chisholm in the quest to recruit the future mothers of Australia. It was highly competitive, and wonderfully successful, especially for the Lang and Chisholm recruits, who were chaperoned carefully on arrival in Australia and placed immediately in employment where they could be assisted and encouraged to be married. By the late 1840s the male-female disparity had been considerably reduced. Mrs Chisholm always referred to her girls as 'God's Police'.

At about the same time a new expression was introduced to Australia. Children born of free parents - and that included the children of Emancipists - began to call themselves 'Currency'. All other free people having a direct connection with Britain, were known as 'Sterling'. There was now a considerable free workforce, so it was not surprising that a movement began amongst the Emancipists and the Currency, to seek to stop any further transportation of convicts. On the other hand the

Exclusives still wanted the unlimited access to convict labour they had always enjoyed. Fierce debates ensued.

Over 50,000 convicts had been sent to Australia between 1815 and 1830. The *Enclosures Act* in Britain had driven poor people to towns, hunger and crime in that precise order. Robert Peel's new police force was very skilful at apprehending criminals, and the gaols were again full to overflowing. Pressure from Australia, however, resulted in the formation of the *Molesworth Committee* of 1838 that recommended an end to transportation. The *Wakefield System*, as instituted in the new colony of South Australia, was held to be the better way to populate Australia. Under that system rich migrants were sold land in Australia prior to embarkation. These migrants used the so-called 'bounty system' to offer assisted passages to 50,000 free labourers and their families, thereby creating a free work force.

The discovery of gold in the late 1830s brought an immense influx of free settlers to Australia over the next 30 years, and the ranks of the 'anti-transportationists' swelled to the point where huge demonstrations were held at Sydney and the new colony of Port Phillip (Melbourne) every time a convict ship arrived. The last convicts to land in Sydney came in 1849. Tasmania received its last consignment of criminals in 1853, but the convict system carried on there until the 1880s when old lags, called 'crawlers' were still working on road gangs around Hobart.

Western Australia, desperate for labour of any background, introduced transportation of convicts in 1850 and retained the system until 1868. At that point it was made clear to the Sandgropers, as West Australians were called, that if they wanted to participate in the eventual Federation of the Australian colonies into a Commonwealth, they must abandon the convict system. The last transported convict in Australia was Samuel Speed, who died in Perth in 1938, aged 84. He had been convicted and transported as a youth for burning a haystack.

God's Police

'Female Emigration to The Great New Southern Nation'
Was the message on the posters, and the passage it was free
So an agonising choice was made by many starving families
Their daughters would be sent across the sea.

"God's Police" said Mrs Chisholm, "that's what their role will be,
We will marry them to all those lawless men
God-fearing girls a plenty, we want for every Colony,
But they'll never, ever, see their home again."

CHORUS
You will never, ever see your home again
You will travel to Australia, to a land of lawless men
The weather and the work will make you old before your time
And you'll never, ever see your home again

Herded in like cattle as the ship ploughed to the south
Seasick and depressed, confused in heart and mind
They tried to keep their spirits up with prayer and speculation
But they'd no idea what type of life they'd find.

"Now, you girls," said Mrs Chisholm, "don't judge this place too fast,
It's nothing like The British Isles, but then,
There's a brand new life that's full of hope for every one of you
But you will never see your home again."

CHORUS
You will never, ever see your home again
etc

There was never any question that all of them would wed
So they did, and they dispersed to different types of fates
With their farmers and their station hands, and men who dug for gold
A motley crew of rough and ready mates.

But the clever Mrs Chisholm had surely chosen well
Their presence was to stabilise the men
They thrived and bore their children and they came to love Australia
But they never, ever saw their home again.

CHORUS
You will never, ever see your home again

Prayers with treacle:
Aboriginals at the mission queue for Bullocky's Joy and other rations

CHAPTER 12

The Sleepy Growth Of The Colonies

> Come and have a little Schluck and a Schnitte with me
> I'll tell you the story of the German families
> Who left their old homeland so they could be free
> They came out to Australia.
>
> Ted Egan, *A Schluck and a Schnitte*

Early in the 19th century exploration of the land was undertaken by agents of the penal colony at Port Jackson, with officers like Major Thomas Mitchell and Captain Charles Sturt prominent. Their focus was on 'the inland sea' that was assumed to exist beyond the coastal mountain range of eastern Australia since the major rivers, the Murray and the Murrumbidgee, flowed in that direction.

After new settlements were established in Van Diemen's Land (1803), Swan River, Perth (1829), Port Phillip (1834) and Adelaide, South Australia (1838) private entrepreneurs encouraged exploration inland, in order that land could be taken up for pastoral and agricultural purposes.

To understand Australia's development it is crucial to know that exploration after 1840 was financed by private individuals and companies. The procedure was straightforward. Explorers traversed the country. They returned to their financial backers with maps, charts, diaries, and detailed reports on the pastoral and agricultural potential of the regions. The financiers went to land offices in London or in the colonial cities, drew arbitrary lines on maps, and applied for land. Almost invariably, allocations of this designated Crown land were granted to the applicants, with rentals and stocking requirements pitched in favour of the new owners, who then sent their representatives to take up the land. Basically the private developers created the rules; the government came along later with police and various other public servants to authenticate the established *modus operandi*.

Hard practices developed in respect of Aboriginals. Those First Australians who opposed settlement were treated as enemies, and conflicts ensued. Those willing to accept the new presence were taken as serf labour. Their land rights were totally disregarded. It was not that their rights were spurned, or ridiculed - in the minds of the new settlers it was inconceivable to contemplate such rights.

In Tasmania, and especially around Hobart, the convict presence was still pervasive. The newer free settlers took up land mainly in the fertile, more temperate north, and charming cities like Launceston, Devonport and Burnie were established. Agriculture and horticulture were easy pastimes in these favoured regions. Sealing and whaling were now important activities in the colder seas to the south of Australia. A desperate group of men, with kidnapped Aboriginal women as partners, provided the work force around the Tasmanian coast and along the Great Australian Bight, for this well-documented and appalling slaughter.

Waves of Migration

In 1788, the population of Australia was probably between 300,000 and 500,000. By 1900 it was about 3 million. At the start of the 21st century it is around 20 million. Since the establishment of the first colony over two hundred years ago, migration has come in a number of waves:

1815-1840 A trickle of free white settlers from Britain
1840-1900 Settlers from Britain and Ireland, many leaving Ireland to escape the Potato Famine, and thousands of single girls and women responding to the Lang and Chisholm campaigns

	Minor groups of white Europeans including Germans to South Australia, Italians to Queensland and Slavs to Western Australia
1850s	Larger numbers of European and Chinese, spurred by the gold rushes
1900-1914	Continuing migration from Britain and, to a lesser extent, continental Europe
1920-1939	Substantial migration from Britain and continental Europe, especially from Italy, Greece and Germany (including refugee Jews)
1947-1960	Huge influx from Displaced Persons camps of Europe. During this time the White Australia policy still prevailed and the term New Australian is introduced
1950-1980	Substantial migration from southern and eastern Europe, especially Italy, Yugoslavia, Poland, Hungary and Greece. Melbourne becomes the second largest Greek city in the world
1960s	Huge British migration under the £10 passage scheme
1980	Substantial Asian migration, often people claiming refugee status from Vietnam, China, Cambodia, Thailand and Indonesia Large migration from New Zealand and smaller numbers from Tonga, Fiji and Samoa as part of population shifts in the Pacific
1990-2000	Substantial family reunification, largely from Asia.

The Northern Territory was too far away to be of any concern to anyone. Successive military settlements between 1824 and 1850 at Fort Dundas, Raffles Bay and Port Essington had seen no invasion from Russia, France, Holland or even Mars. The soldiers and convicts had died from fever or spear wounds from the pesky Aboriginals, who seemed to take the stance that the land was theirs and that they would remain in charge. 'Leave it to them. It's what they deserve'. The North was abandoned by South Australia in 1911, and became a Federal Territory. Its day is about to dawn. Since World War II great pioneering work has been done to establish formidable mining, pastoral, horticultural and tourism industries.

Western Australia took a long time to develop the independent spirit it now enjoys. The settlers, under the socalled sponsorship of Thomas Peel, and with the authority of Governor James Stirling, landed on the beach in 1829 at what is now fashionable Fremantle surrounded by their fancy furniture, grand pianos and roll-top desks, they were appalled at the desolation, the flies, and the sterile, sandy soil. They were to wallow in their ineptitude for the next 20 years, until they were granted permission to introduce convict labour. Things did not improve much even then. The Swan River settlement seemed destined to wither away. But slowly, independence emerged; gold and other minerals were discovered, impressive cereal crops were grown, huge cattle and sheep stations were established, especially in the north, and pearls were found in the bountiful tropical waters. The Sandgropers eventually challenged the Eastern staters or 'the wise men from the east' in every feature of colonial life.

Port Phillip, later Victoria, with its capital Melbourne on the sparkling Yarra River, was declared by John Batman to be 'the spot for a village' and was settled from Tasmania in the 1830s. Probably the worst of all of Australia's black/white contact periods began in this new colony. The British settlers in Tasmania had come to believe that it was desirable to eliminate the Aboriginals. In Victoria they knew from the outset what had to be done, and they went to their task of clearing the land of the human vermin with an appalling zeal. The Whyte brothers set themselves a quota they termed 'fifty niggers a week' in Western Victoria. The surviving natives were herded onto mission stations and placed on a diet of flour, treacle ('Bullocky's Joy') and Jesus. Their land was gone; but surely salvation was at hand? Gold was discovered. The self-styled Garden State flourished. The few surviving Aboriginals became benign objects of

"Mine Tinkit They Fit"

Smart casual: Aboriginals were used in poster campaigns in Victoria to promote dress shirts

ridicule, perfect for advertising Pelaco shirts: "Mine tinkit they fit", was the message on the hoardings.

In 1838, South Australia was occupied by free settlers under the Wakefield System. From the outset, convicts were not in the equation. A remarkable experiment, with many benign consequences for Australia, saw the arrival of a few hundred German settlers from Silesia, now part of Poland. These victims of religious persecution in their homeland settled in what they saw as the 'Valleys of Hope' of South Australia - the Barossa and Hahndorf. They remained true to their Lutheran beliefs and practices, and proved to be just the type of farmers Australia needed. Stay put, dig deep, work hard. And a bit of fun is not out of the question.

> They started up their farms, they battled with the land
> The freedom was free, the life it was grand
> The old songs were sung to an oom-pa-pah band
> And the church bells rang out in the Valley.
>
> Komm und hab einen kleinen Schluck und Schnitte mit mir
> Ich erzahle die Geschichte von Deutschen Familien
> Sie verliezhen ihr Heimatland, nun sind sie frei
> Und leben in Australien.
>   Ted Egan, *Schluck und Schnitte*

Queensland was also slow to develop, from the original penal colony at Moreton Bay, northward along the coast. The terrain was rough, the weather was hot, and the southern markets hard to reach. Splendid provincial towns were established along the coastline, and railways were threaded inland to access the mineral and pastoral potential. Slowly, expertise in tropical agriculture and horticulture was acquired, and large areas of sugar, pineapples and mangoes were grown. Labour for these enterprises was provided by the 'blackbirding' of people from the Pacific Islands, who were kidnapped and brought to Australia under indentures. Called 'Kanakas', they were to become one of the least recognised of the many pioneer ethnic groups who took the tropical north into eventual prosperity through sheer hard work.

There were those who already advocated a White Australia policy. To counter the movement of Kanaka and other 'coolie' labour to north Australia, and at the same time show that the white man could indeed survive and work in the tropics, a concerted move brought a significant migration of Italians to develop sugar and tobacco plantations in north Queensland. That move was successful. Fortunately Italians and Kanakas lived, and still live, in harmony in the region. Hard workers, great citizens.

Bullocky's Joy & Jesus

Once upon a time, doing fine
Living in the bush, blackfeller way
Kids all laughing, Mum and Dad hunting,
No worries, no rent to pay.

Then the whitefellers came to stay
Said they'd show us where we went wrong
Said they'd teach us a better way
They taught us to sing a Jesus song.

CHORUS
Bullocky's Joy and Jesus, boy,
That's the only way to go
Bullocky's Joy and Jesus, boy,
The Bible tells me so.

Leave the bush, come to the Mission
Can't go naked, much too rude
Girls get dresses, boys get cockrags
Learn to eat the whitefeller food.

Ring the bell, go to school
Teach us all the Golden Rule,
Sewing, gardening, everything,
And God save our Gracious King.

Bullocky's Joy and Jesus, boy etc.

Line up all you Christian darkies
Manners now, say "Thank you" Jacky
Here's your flour, tea and sugar,
Bullocky's Joy and black terbaccy.

Shout "Hooray" on Blanket Day
That's the day the whitefellers pay
We should be grateful, so they say,
Pays for the land they took away.

Bullocky's Joy and Jesus, boy etc

Guts get fat, teeth all stuffed
Whitefeller tucker, make you sick
Social Service, can't go bush,
Flagon of plonk might do the trick.

The miners said: "We'd like this land".
The Government said: "We'll give you a hand
It's Government land, didn't you know?
The blackfellers left there long ago"

Bullocky's Joy and Jesus, boy
That's the only way to go
Bullocky's Joy and Jesus, boy,
The Bible tells me so.

There is a a happy land, far, far away
Where saints in glory stand, bright, bright as day
No sugar in our tea, bread and butter we never see,
That's why we're gradually....fading away
Amen.

Preparing to die: Bushranger Ned Kelly the day before he was hanged
By permission of La Trobe Picture Collection, State Library of Victoria

CHAPTER 13

Explorers, Gold, Bushrangers, Eureka

> You robbed the banks,
> You played some pranks
> Dodged in and out the scrub
> Euroa, then Jerilderie
> Then Glenrowan at Jones's Pub
> But a telegram to Melbourne,
> Brought the traps, and there's the rub
> Such is life, Ned Kelly,
> Such is life.
>
> **Ted Egan,** *Such is Life*

Gold! Gold! Gold! First near Bathurst, New South Wales in 1838. Then, in the 1850s in the Ballarat and Bendigo regions of Victoria, it was discovered at bonanza level. Huge nuggets of reef gold and alluvial gold. Literally, tons of it. Hundreds of thousands of newcomers from all points of the globe found their way to Port Phillip. Melbourne was transformed from a collection of tents and humpies into an economic metropolis, with banks and hotels on every corner. Ballarat and Bendigo were built from scratch to become two of the finest cities in the world. Nothing was too good for the diggers. They lit their cigars with five pound notes. They saw Lola Montez dance. They drank the best wines at Craig's and other fine hotels. The finest blood horses were imported. In other countries horseracing was the exclusive 'sport of Kings'. "But we're all kings in Australia", said the diggers.

At first it was not so rosy on the goldfields. In easy-going societies like Australia, bureaucracy often triumphs. The colonial government was quick to introduce strict, uncompromising licensing laws and regulations to control who dug the gold and where, and to enable the Crown to share in the profits. Licensing police were sent to collect the requisite fees from the diggers. Many of the new arrivals to the gold fields of Australia had come from California. Most diggers carried firearms and displayed a certain disregard for authority. Under the leadership of Peter Lalor, the diggers combined and refused to pay the licence fees, on the principle of 'no taxation without representation'. The government authorities were unimpressed, and many arrests were made.

Australia came the closest it has ever been to civil war in December 1854 when 150 diggers at Ballarat enclosed themselves in a crude compound that they called The Eureka Stockade. Their flag of blue and silver stars, based on the constellation *Crux Australis*, the Southern Cross, flew in the breeze.

New Labour: Miners' leader Peter Lalor, MLA, says
'No taxation without representation'
By permission of the National Archives of Australia

It was no contest. The diggers were armed with a few muskets and pikes. The 300 soldiers were highly organised, aggressive, hostile, mounted and heavily armed. In a confrontation lasting only a couple of hours, 30 diggers were killed, 50 wounded and 13 imprisoned on charges of high treason. Only five troopers were killed.

The imprisoned diggers were acquitted, as no jury was prepared to declare them guilty. Although the fight was lost, their principle was established. The formidable Lalor, who had lost an arm in the battle, demanded, and got, dialogue with Governor Charles Hotham. Miners Rights costing £1 replaced licences, and the holders of Miners Rights won the right to vote in Legislative Council elections. Lalor became a very effective politician in the new colonial government.

Gold and crime are always bedmates, and significant numbers of bushrangers appeared, staging hold-ups and robberies in Victoria and New South Wales, on a scale probably not equalled even in the American West. On the Australian frontier, all men carried arms.

Bushranging in Australia saw three periods. The first bushranger was an escaped Jamaican convict, Black Caesar, who stole foodstuffs from Governor Phillip's work parties, until he was caught and hanged. Later, and especially in Tasmania, escaped convicts like Matthew Brady and 'Bold Jack' Donohue made raids and holdups more to embarrass officialdom than for any other purpose. By and large, the convict 'bolters' were romantic figures.

In the goldrush days, robbery was the principal motive, and figures like 'Darky' Gardiner, Jackey Jackey, Captain Thunderbolt, Captain Moonlight and the gallant Ben Hall 'bailed up' coaches and individual travellers, incurring the wrath of the colonial authorities.

Ned Kelly is Australia's best known, and most-debated bushranger. He was a member of an Irish settler family subjected to constant harassment by a police force that had many corrupt officers within its ranks. Kelly was representative of a body of Irish Catholics who took to the road in this, the third, phase of Australian bushranging, and engaged in thefts of livestock and money in the face of sectarian brutality by a police force guided and dominated by the Freemason establishment.

Kelly is the subject of many films, books, plays, poems - and songs. The world's first full-length feature film was made about Ned Kelly, in Australia. Was he a cold-blooded murderer or a freedom fighter?

Administering the oath: Eureka Stockade 1854
By permission of La Trobe Picture Collection, State Library of Victoria

In 1878 Kelly and his gang, consisting of his brother Dan, Steve Hart and Joe Byrne, fought and killed three policemen at Stringybark Creek. He then embarked on a campaign of bank robberies at Euroa, Jerilderie and Glenrowan, and in each case the folklore evolved around his manners, chivalry and intelligence. He wrote a famous *Letter from Jerilderie* addressed to the authorities-at-large; there is hot debate to this day whether it is the literary work of a madman or a prophet.

In his final confrontation in 1880 with a train-load of policeman at Glenrowan, in north-east Victoria, Kelly clad himself in ploughshare armour and walked to his fate confronting the police and firing two revolvers. He was eventually downed by the police, nursed to health, and taken to Melbourne for trial. There he conducted a spirited defence of his own actions, but a gleeful Judge Barry sentenced him to death. Asked by the Judge if he had anything to say, Kelly confronted his tormenter with the challenge to see him soon - in Hell. Kelly was hanged on 11 November 1880, aged 25. The Judge died inexplicably soon afterwards. Kelly's last words before the drop of the trapdoor at Pentridge Gaol in Melbourne were "Such is life". The mythology continues, the speculation abounds.

> They took you down to Melbourne
> Where you copped the legal rage
> Such is life, Ned Kelly, such is life
> November 1880, twenty-five years of age
> Such is life, Ned Kelly, such is life
> They sentenced you to hanging
> They dragged you up in chains
> They hung you by the neck
> They mutilated your remains
> But they didn't know that martyrdom
> A hero's life sustains
> Such is life, Ned Kelly, such is life.
>
> Ted Egan, *Such is Life*

Always riding further out: Drover Bill Gwydir on the Birdsville Track.
Picture by permission of the artist, Robert Wettenhall

CHAPTER 14

Old Bluey & The Intrepid Scot

> "My father opened up more of Australia than any of the explorers."
>
> Gordon Buchanan, *Packhorse and Waterhole*

The discovery of gold and the huge population influx which followed strengthened the pastoral, agricultural, mining and horticultural bases of Australia. In their new-found egalitarianism, primary industry workers were less inclined than formerly to 'tug the forelock'. More and more land was taken up for primary industry. By 1860 there were 40 million sheep in Australia. The ships that brought migrants to Australia were back-loaded with the incomparable merino wool - the 'golden fleece'.

> Shear the golden fleece, boys,
> Shear the golden fleece,
> From anywhere to back o' Bourke,
> Shear the golden fleece.

More and more pastoral land was required. The government explorers of the early 19th century had dispelled the notion that there must be a huge inland sea and appurtenant fertile country in central Australia. The large Queensland rivers flowing inland from northern regions were found to merge into the Cooper, and on into Lake Eyre, a vast salt lake below sea level, the principal feature of a sterile basin. The New South Wales inland rivers, the Lachlan, Darling, and Murrumbidgee merged with the Murray to meander into Lake Alexandrina, and thence to the Great Southern Ocean.

Overlanders' routes

Large farm and station properties were quickly established along all of these freshwater inland rivers. Brutal exploitation of the land commenced, through ringbarking of forests and total clearing for wattle bark. There was unchecked irrigation, and heavy stocking of cloven-footed animals, with little or no thought that such practices must eventually leach and salinate the fragile soil. One hundred and fifty years later Australia is desperately trying to correct the follies of our forefathers, pampered as they were by politicians who manipulated and maintained tremendous political clout for 'the man on the land'.

It was always too easy for governments to adopt a benign attitude, as settlers were encouraged to take up marginal land, clear it, and then endure abject poverty as they battled to make a living. No wonder the poorer farmers came to be known as 'cockies' - the only creatures that seemed to thrive in the cleared Mallee scrub were the cockatoos, who feasted and multiplied on the seed sown on land never meant to be farmed.

That is not to denigrate all farming in Australia. In the better regions, magnificent farming skills have developed and Australia can match the world in terms of farming techniques, inventions and land management. It is just that there is too much farming in areas that should never have been developed in the first place, areas that must cease to be farmed in the near future. Along all the river frontages there is chaos and deplorable diminution of fragile, sensitive land. Most rivers are wrecked, and will only recover with implementation of sound restoration policies.

Into the more remote northern and western regions went the explorers Leichhardt, McDouall Stuart, Burke and Wills, Lindsay, the Forrest brothers, Gregory, McKinlay, Jardine, Cunningham, Oxley, and Eyre. Wherever the explorers provided favourable reports the rich landholders of southern Australia and far-off England besieged the land offices in London, Sydney, Melbourne, Brisbane, Adelaide and Perth. Politicians like 'Free Selection Jack' Robertson introduced the principle that an average farm should be 640 acres in area. In more arid, remote areas, grazing land for sheep and cattle was taken up in the form of huge stations, with properties averaging 1,000 square miles. Because the land was marginal and distances to markets were long and hazardous, it was felt that only huge holdings could succeed. Some of the grants of Crown land were larger than countries in Europe. One single property, Victoria River Downs Station (VRD, as it came to be called) was 50,000 square miles and eventually ran 300,000 head of cattle.

From 1880 onwards the biggest movements of cattle the world had ever seen took place, as the overlanders walked mobs, totalling hundreds of thousands, to stock 'the big runs'. It was the squattocracy who owned the land: but it was the working class who walked the cattle, men and women, black and white.

Led at the outset by the legendary Nat Buchanan, huge mobs of cattle were herded across thousands of miles into unknown country. In one single movement in 1882, Buchanan safely escorted 20,000 head of cattle over 2500 miles to set up Northern Territory and Kimberley stations. The Duracks, Costellos, Kilfoyles and McDonalds followed, to establish family-owned dynasties and a strong Celtic influence in the more remote regions.

In 1890, a minor goldrush to Hall's Creek, in the Kimberley gave the new pastoralists a healthy beef market for a short time, but the overseas markets they hoped to set up in the East Indies (Indonesia), Malaya (Malaysia) and The Philippines did not eventuate. So began a process of walking the progeny from the big northern stations back to southern markets. For the next 80 years the drovers walked the cattle, in mobs averaging 1200 head, from 'anywhere' to 'wherever' along the various stock routes.

> Time and distance don't mean a thing
> Our bullocks are feeding, slow,
> Twelve hundred head, and they're all scrub-bred
> And they carry the O-Five-O *
>
> Ted Egan, *The Wave Hill Track* (chorus)
> * O-Five-O is the brand of Ord River Station, Western Australia.

A word put into common usage in Australia during the exploring and overlanding days was 'depot'. The more astute explorers like John McDouall Stuart and the better overlanders like the admirable Nat Buchanan, never took risks with the lives of either their men or their stock. In their travels they would establish a depot where there was adequate feed and water for their stock. As leaders, they felt it was their personal responsibility to ride ahead to find the location of the next depot. Only then would they permit forward progress.

McDouall Stuart was a Scot who had worked as a surveyor under another great explorer, Charles Sturt. In 1860 a competition was announced offering a reward for the first person or group to traverse Australia successfully from south to north. A route was being sought to enable a telegraph line to be erected across the continent, and link up with a cable to be laid under the ocean to Singapore, thereby connecting Australia with Europe telegraphically.

The colony of Victoria financed Burke and Wills, whose elaborately equipped party set out from Melbourne to great acclamation. They were thought to be invincible. Camels had been introduced to Australia to help open up the inland, and the

Buchanan was king: the world's most famous drover
Bronze sculpture by Eddie Hackman

Burke and Wills party used these wonderful beasts both for riding and as pack animals. They passed through mainly settled country, staying at station homesteads for most of their journey, until they entered north-western Queensland. They did manage to reach the northern coastline on the Gulf of Carpentaria, but on their return journey perished at Cooper's Creek. The party had been totally inept in most of its undertakings. To die of hunger at bountiful Cooper's Creek, having eaten their camels, and in spite of being surrounded by water and friendly Aboriginals, was the final folly.

McDouall Stuart set out with minor fanfare from Adelaide, and over the next five years had four failures, each time returning to Adelaide rather than risking the life of his party. On these occasions it was because he could not establish the next depot, or there was threat of Aboriginal attack, or, in one case, he encountered impenetrable lancewood scrub near what is today Daly Waters. Eventually Stuart reached the northern coastline at a point later called (by others) Point Stuart. The intrepid Scot always, in his articulate diary entries, paid tribute to his men, and to "my pretty grey mare, Polly," who carried him thousands of miles on the five attempts. On the final return trip his health deteriorated, and his men fashioned a rough drag stretcher, to which he was tied for the last few hundred miles into Adelaide. Stuart was acclaimed as a hero on return to South Australia, but his health never recovered. He elected to return to England where he died in 1866, a shattered man and aged only 50. The reward was never paid to him. He is buried at Kensal Green in London. By 1872 the Overland Telegraph Line was erected in the pathway he had mapped. Australia was linked to the rest of the world.

Nathaniel Buchanan was born in Ireland but came to Australia with his family at the age of six. As a young man he was a stockman and a butcher, but then went to California for the gold rush. He found no gold but he had learnt one big lesson in America: men on goldfields need meat. When he returned to Australia at the start of the gold rushes he set up as a cattle drover and established a considerable reputation. He was asked to take cattle into western Queensland where he became a member of a group called the Landsborough Five - their brand was the famous LC5 - which set up the important Bowen Downs Station, soon to become a depot in the north western cattle droving scene. In 1863 he brought his bride, Kitty, to Bowen Downs; she was the first white woman in the region. Their marriage was to be a very devoted one, and it also established the beginning of another important association for Buchanan - with Kitty's brothers, the Gordons. After ten years of droving and mining in north Queensland, Nat Buchanan was commissioned in 1877 to take cattle to Rocklands Station, on the Queensland-Northern Territory border, and on the edge of the magnificent Barkly Tableland. Seemingly endless treeless plains were covered with Mitchell and Flinders grass, perfect for grazing cattle. The country between Rocklands and the

Overland Telegraph line - 600 miles as the crow flies - was heavily grassed, but there was no permanent water. Buchanan knew that in order to take cattle to the Kimberley in Western Australia, the other important region for cattle, he would have to follow the coastal track negotiated by the German explorer Leichhardt in the 1840s.

Rider in the mirage: signed portrait of John McDouall Stuart, who set the route for Australia's first telegraph.
By permission of the National Library of Australia

From 1880 to 1900, following this track time and again, Buchanan earned a deserved reputation as the greatest cattle drover the world has ever seen, and arguably Australia's greatest ever bushman. He established huge Northern Territory 'top end runs' like Glencoe, Victoria River Downs and Wave Hill. In Western Australia he helped establish cattle stations from the Ord River (Kimberley) region down to the Murchison. On his largest droving trip he walked 20,000 head from Queensland to Glencoe, a distance of 2,500 miles. Imagine the logistics. North America has nothing in its history to match such feats.

Nat Buchanan had two nicknames. White people called him 'Bluey'. In those days in Australia you were called Bluey if you had blue (grey) hair. Today in Australia, for some inexplicable reason, you are called Bluey or Blue if you have auburn (red) hair. In many cases Buchanan was the first white man some Aboriginal groups had ever seen. They came to call him 'Paraway'. To avoid confrontation with Aboriginal groups, whom he respected and from whom he learnt a lot of his bush skills, Buchanan would always gesticulate to indicate that he did not want to take over or stay on their land. Something like: "I have come from *far away*, and I want to travel *far away*". As there is no 'f' sound in most Australian languages, Aboriginals assumed 'Paraway' must be his name. It is the practice among Aboriginals for a stranger to establish immediately an identity for a stranger. Something like: "Ngaiyu bana yanandjara Balggu: ngaiyu Jabangardi", which means "I come from Balggu: my name is Jabangardi".

There are two fine books about Buchanan, *Packhorse and Waterhole* by his son Gordon Buchanan, and *In the Tracks of Old Bluey* by his great-granddaughter Bobbie Buchanan. Gordon Buchanan says with some justification: "My father opened up more of Australia than any of the explorers". Nat Buchanan died and was buried at Tamworth in 1901, aged 76. Later his remains were exhumed so he could be reburied alongside his beloved wife Catherine (Kitty) at Walcha, New South Wales.

Rider In The Mirage

An ancient man of fifty died
In the soft, green English countryside
A place called Kensal Green
The people in the village tried to speculate
On what he'd done and where he might have been
The children of the village all made fun
They laughed at him, no matter where he went
His eyes a stare, a shock of hair
His body bent, his skin all gnarled and rent

CHORUS

John McDouall Stuart, rider in the mirage
John McDouall Stuart with his tiny entourage
On his pretty grey mare, Polly,
In the burning sand and sun,
Intrepid man, number one.

Five times McDouall Stuart tried
But at every turn he was defied
By salt and sandy piles
His faithful Kekwick by his side
It seemed like an eternal ride
Ten thousand weary miles
The steel-shod desert drove him back
He floundered to and fro, and Polly reeled
But back again, and then again
Determined still, he vowed he'd never yield

CHORUS
John McDouall Stuart etc

The Kaititj tribesmen drove him back
Bewildered nomads in attack
Red desert men of old
But back he came to try again
Through the lancewood scrub and the open plain
This Scot was truly bold
His body wracked with fever
He fought with death, postponed it for a day
And finally he battled through
McDouall Stuart and gallant crew
And Polly, all the way.

King Paraway

In the 80's Australia saw movements of cattle
In the world's driest continent, the drovers did battle
With Nature and thousands of hard miles were spanned
Hundreds of thousands walked overland
Into Queensland, the Territory, the Kimberley runs
In the forefront, one of the land's finest sons
There are hundreds of drovers of whom we can sing
And everyone knows Nat Buchanan was King.

CHORUS
Nat Buchanan, old Bluey, old Paraway
What would you think if you came back today?
It's not as romantic as in your time, old Nat,
Not many drovers, and we're sad about that.
Fences, bitumen, road trains galore
They move cattle quicker, but one thing is sure
Road trains go faster, but of drovers we sing
And everyone knows Nat Buchanan was King.

The bush blacks all called him Old Paraway
You see him tomorrow, he left yesterday,
With thousand of cattle he keeps riding on
To nowhere, from somewhere,
Here he comes, now he's gone
With a bright green umbrella to shade the fierce sun
On the Murranji, the Murchison, another new run
Paraway's the man of whom desert tribes sing
And everyone knows Nat Buchanan was King.

People talk about drovers, and who was the best
Some give you their choice, and discard all the rest
There are books on the subject with hundreds of pages
Of bullocks that rushed, and the endless dry stages
Old timers regale you with tales of the past
Of whipping up water, and night horses fast
There are hundreds of drovers of whom we could sing
And everyone knows Nat Buchanan was King.

If drovers had titles Bill Gwydir's a Prince
None better at Birdsville, before him or since
Matt Savage would be Duke of the Murranji Track
Edna Zigenbine the Queen of the plains way out back
Arch McLean, Ted Sheehan, old Walter Rose,
They'd be Knights of The Saddle, as everyone knows
There are hundreds of drovers of whom we could sing
And everyone knows Nat Buchanan was King.

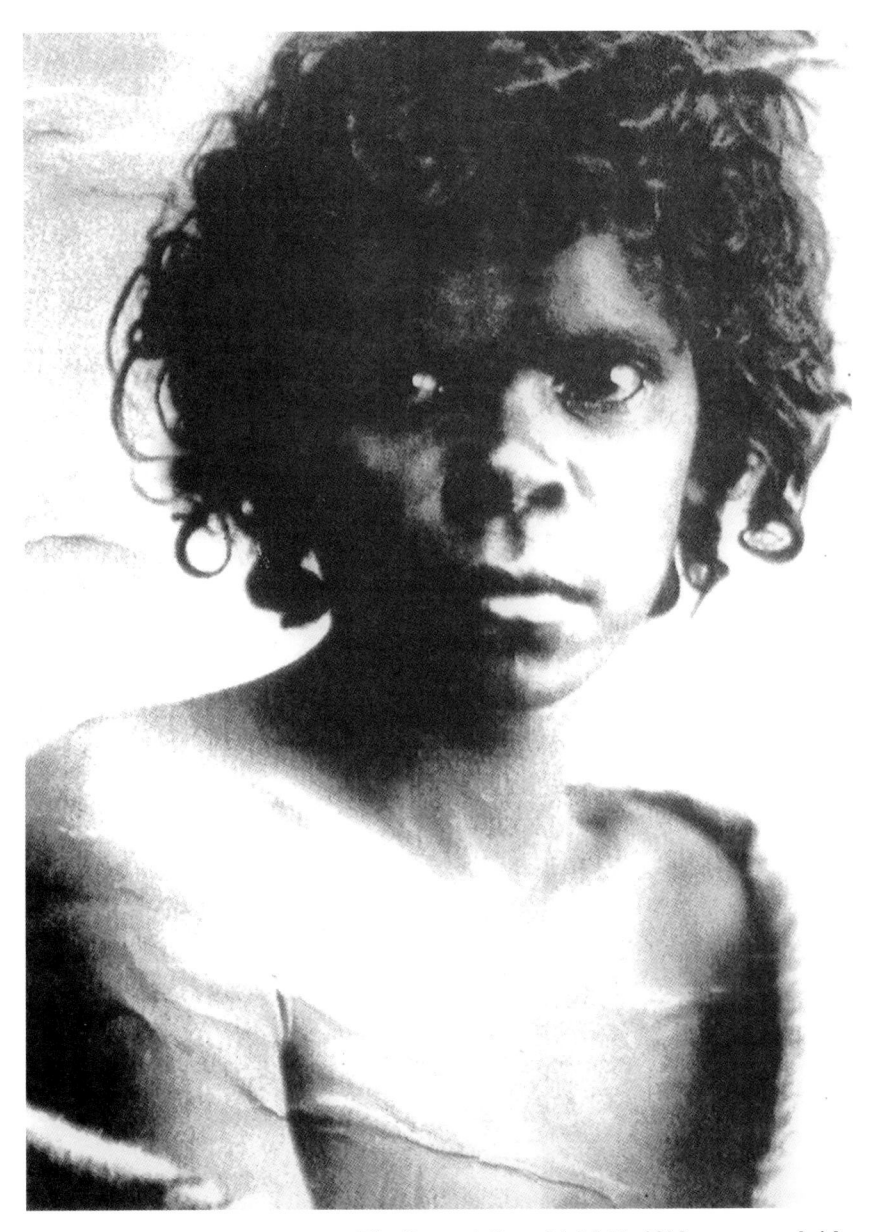

The Drover's Boy: faithful 'wife' but never a bride.
Photo: Department of Aboriginal Affairs

CHAPTER 15

The Overlanders, Drover's Boys, & Other Women Pioneers

> **Further out, we're the Overlanders**
> **Riding further out**
> **We're undeterred, by fire, flood and drought**
> **As we take up each selection**
> **There's a constant predilection**
> **To head in the right direction**
> **Further out.**
>
> **Ted Egan, *Further Out*, 1981**

The movements of cattle into northern regions of Australia, from around 1860 and peaking in the 1880s, were to have profound effects on the lifestyle of the many Aboriginal groups that had inhabited the country for countless thousands of centuries without any human threat to their existence. There were important factors present at the point of first contact in the north that were different from similar situations elsewhere in Australia. In the remote regions the Aboriginals for many years outnumbered the whites. The Aboriginals were very efficient hunters, and slow-moving cattle presented an easy target for spearmen who could hit a kangaroo on the run at 80 metres. However, the whites by this time had very superior firearms. The Martini-Henry rifle was, according to the notorious Constable Henry Willshire, "perfect for teaching English to the blacks".

There was often conflict. No white death went unavenged. There is ongoing dispute about the numbers killed on both sides, but there is little doubt that there were many more Aboriginals who died from bullets, or more insidiously, from eating poisoned flour or 'pink' sugar (laced with strychnine) handed to them as 'gifts', than there were whites speared or clubbed to death. Many of the overlanders took trained southern Aboriginals with them to match the skills of the bush blacks, the so called Munjongs. Some of these 'enforcers' established awesome and awful reputations as executioners. 'Clearing the land' took on serious, sinister connotations. In northwest Queensland zealous white killers like Sub-Inspector Urquhart led the nefarious Native Police, a group of Aboriginal men recruited and trained to hunt down and eliminate their countrymen. White police often used some old tribal grievance, or the offer of captured girls or women, as an incentive to their traitorous, salacious troopers.

There were nonetheless, in post-conflict situations, large movements by Aboriginals who chose to work for the whites in almost feudal conditions. In return for some of the white man's commodities, particularly beef, flour, tea, sugar, tobacco and clothing, the Aboriginals became menial labourers. Because whites generally had no interest in Aboriginals other than for exploitation, this lifestyle often had almost a positive outcome for Aboriginals, especially if there was 'a good boss' or, better still, 'a good missus'. Even if the whites were uncaring, exploitative or cruel, traditional life went on 'in the camp' alongside the western system. 'Pidgin' English became the working *lingua franca*, but among the Aboriginals themselves old languages were spoken, ceremonies were performed, kinship rules were obeyed and the vital contact with the land was retained. Aboriginal stockmen and women could visit sacred sites and perform ceremonial obligations on horseback, as part of the job of mustering the cattle. Considerable skills were acquired in cattle work and in all related activities around the cattle stations, which were in effect small, independent, isolated townships. If something went wrong, somebody fixed it. Everybody from the oldest pensioner to the smallest child had a role to fulfil.

There were very few white women on the Australian frontier in the early years. Rape and sexual exploitation of Aboriginal women was a way of life for many white men. Many white men acquired a 'stud' - a black girl who was required to 'work all day on a horse and work all night in the 'swag'. In most cases it was straight-out kidnapping, rape, and slavery, often accompanied by brutal treatment. There were few exceptions where a meaningful relationship developed and mixed-race children were recognised by their white fathers, but more often than not a woman would be exploited as long as she was considered useful or attractive, and then discarded. The more fortunate of them returned to their people, where their mixed race children might be given an identity and perhaps marry a person of full descent. More likely, as 'yeller fellers', the children would be removed to an institution if they came under the scrutiny of the police, or were an embarrassment to their white fathers who often assumed great local respectability as they became older and richer, surrounded by their legitimate white offspring (see Chapter 10).

Laws were eventually passed in all states and in the Northern Territory to 'protect' Aboriginal people from themselves and potential adversaries. Their every movement could be prescribed by the appointed Chief Protectors of Aboriginals. Aboriginals were denied the right to move freely, drink alcohol, vote or be registered to vote, marry without permission, be in towns between sunset and sunrise, or co-habit with non-Aboriginals. White people who wished to employ, marry, or otherwise be in contact with Aboriginals required a licence from the Chief Protector. Mandatory three-to-six month prison sentences were prescribed for whites who failed to comply with the law. Aboriginals who offended were usually punished by commital to their own or somebody else's tribal country for a period like six months - but there are on record many instances where Aboriginal people were banished from their own tribal areas for life.

The white police expected to enforce the law usually had sympathy with the white party in these matters, so the prosecution of white men was often a selective practice: a 'nudge-nudge, wink-wink' attitude allowed them to keep their 'studs'. Policemen themselves were often the fathers of mixed-race children.

The Aboriginals Ordinance was introduced into the Northern Territory in 1911 when the Federal Government took control of that region. One of the sections of the Ordinance prescribed that 'female Aboriginals' were not allowed to be employed as cattle drovers or taken from their tribal areas. Often, in remote frontier areas, girls taken as 'studs' by white men, were masqueraded as males. They wore trousers, shirts, and hats, and they did the same work as men, droving cattle. Their hair was cut short, and they were given 'whitefeller' names like Jimmy, Paddy, Jacky.

Drovers "Boys" Alexandria Station, Northern Territory, 1916.

In the Northern Territory in later years it became a great source of fun for old Aboriginal women to recount, often in lurid detail, their experiences with white men. The sexual prowess of their white masters was analysed in explicit terms. Many laughed as they recalled having several different whitefeller names in their associations with white men. Often they would talk about life on cattle stations before the white boss eventually conformed with society's demands and took his white wife. "One time we all Mrs Johnson here," reminisced one old Aboriginal lady who was known as Billy Johnson when she was a drover's boy for Mr Johnson.

While the employment of those women and girls was in most cases total exploitation, many of them looked back with considerable nostalgia on what had often been exciting times. It was no tougher than their normal role of hunters and gatherers in the traditional manner. Certainly they deserve to be honoured for their part in the history of Australia, as participants in the great cattle movements of the time.

As previously noted, there were few white women on the extreme frontier in north Australia, but it must not be thought that only white men and selected Aboriginals participated in the country's development. From convict days to the present time women of all backgrounds and races have been wonderful contributors in all phases of Australian life.

It is certainly true to say that Australia is 'a man's country' mainly because life has been so much easier for white men. Men made the rules, they wrote the Constitution and they prescribed the roles. The Inter-Colonial Conferences of the 1880s were led by the redoubtable Sir Henry Parkes. Thus evolved the Federation of the States, the creation of the Commonwealth, the introduction of the Australian Constitution and the establishment of a Federal Parliament. Only men attended those conferences: almost all of them were over 60 years of age. Flowing beards were all the rage.

Women by and large conformed, putting up with hardships men would not and could not tolerate. In the main, women stayed sober, bore their children - often in the most dangerous of situations - and endured loneliness, poverty and brutality. The men of Australia had more interesting lives. Mobility has always been available to them, even in the tough times of Depression, and especially in the exciting times created by overseas wars. The much-vaunted Australian 'mateship' is a wonderful but usually essentially male phenomenon, where Australian men look after one another. The mateship among women was always there, but was more real, more altruistic than the male, back-scratching variety. Until recent years, the women of Australia had little

Dame Mary Gilmore (1865-1962) is a national identity for her pursuit of social justice, literature and her love of rural Australia. She was honoured by King George VI for her work among the rural poor and her face is on $10 notes and stamps
Eric Saunders portrait by permission of the National Library of Australia

choice in job selection, were not given easy admission to the professions and trades, and were denied equality in any matter of consequence.

At the same time it must not be thought that Australian women were or are subservient wimps. Along with their New

Zealand cousins, Australian women were the first in the world to demand, and get, the right to vote. There is a characteristic openness and determination in many Australian girls and women that allows them to be achievers against the odds, and in most cases to be better in crises than Australian men. This has manifested itself in all walks of life, and especially in sport, where so many Australian 'golden girls' have excelled. For every Boy from Bowral there is a Lithgow Flash.

Old Ned

They reckon Old Ned is too stiff to be riding
Too old at the stockyards, when the drafting is done
His eyesight is shot, for the tracking and the guiding,
He'll muster no more, with the camp, on the run.

Let him dream on, let the old bloke remember
The days when he rode, where the wild cattle were
Pension him off, but just let him cherish
Memories of stockwhip, stirrup and spur.

In his day there were few who could stay there beside him
Through the gidyea and the wattle, when swinging the lead
Few horses could throw him, no man could outride him
The best in the Gulf, the old timers agreed.

Let him dream on, etc

Let's yarn to Old Ned in his camp by the river
Far from the hills that were mustered back then
The legendary stockman, it's sad that he'll never
Go running the pikers and the cleanskins again.

Let him dream on, etc.

They reckon Old Ned is too stiff to be a riding
Too old at the stockyards when the drafting is done
His eyesight is shot, for the tracking and the guiding
He'll muster no more, with the camp, on the run.

The Drover's Boy

They couldn't understand why the drover cried
As they buried The Drover's Boy
For the drover had always seemed so hard
To the men in his employ
A bolting horse, a stirrup lost
And The Drover's Boy was dead
The shovelled dirt, a mumbled word
And it's back to the road ahead
And forget about The Drover's Boy

They couldn't understand why the drover cut
A lock of the dead Boy's hair
He put it in the band of his battered old hat
As they watched him standing there,
He told them, "Take the cattle on,
I'll sit with The Boy a while"
A silent thought, a pipe to smoke
Then it's ride another mile,
And forget about The Drover's Boy

They couldn't understand why the drover and The Boy
Always camped so far away
For the tall white man and the slim black Boy
Had never had much to say
The Boy would be gone at break of dawn
Tail the horses, carry on,
While the drover roused the sleeping men,
"Daylight, hit the road again,
And follow, The Drover's Boy
Follow The Drover's Boy".

In the Camooweal Pub they talked about
The death of The Drover's Boy
They drank their rum with a stranger who'd come
From a Kimberley run, Fitzroy,
He told of the massacre in the west
Barest detail, guess the rest,
Shoot the bucks, grab a gin,
Cut her hair, break her in
And call her a boy, The Drover's Boy
Call her a boy, The Drover's Boy

So when they build that Stockman's Hall of Fame
And they talk about the droving game
Remember the girl who was bedmate and guide,
Rode with the drover, side by side
Watched the bullocks, flayed the hide
Faithful wife, but never a bride
Bred his sons for the cattle runs,
Don't weep, for The Drover's Boy
Don't mourn, for The Drover's Boy,
But don't forget The Drover's Boy.

Alyandabu

Straight out of a Drysdale canvas you walked
Down Vesteys Hill
Past the Government Gardens
And right on, into town.
Straight as a spear shaft
Wide-brimmed hat
Tall and proud and black
It's one of the many roads that you've walked down.

CHORUS
And I wonder what you're thinking about
As you walk on through your life?
Are you thinking about the Irishman
Who took you as his wife?
Or the kids you bore?
The things you saw?
The hard times you were made to endure?
What's your story, Alyandabu?

When you were young you saw your tribe wiped out
All your people killed,
Poisoned flour and bullets were their fate.
But you survived
And in your life
A laughing Irishman arrived
You both shared a life that knew no hate.

You found the famous Lucy Mine
Worked it with your man
Raised five kids, but then disaster came.
McGinness died
Officials tried
To take your children from you
They wanted both your family and your claim.

Into Darwin town you came
Fighting for your rights
Battling to keep your family by your side
Today you'd be so fond of them
Descendants by the score
You taught them all about a thing called pride.

If you were white, they'd call you a pioneer
Name a suburb after you
But you're forgotten by the ones who took your land.
But those who knew you,
Knew your worth
Cherish private thoughts
And memories strangers couldn't understand.

So I wonder what you're thinking about
As you walk on through your life?
Are you thinking about the Irishman
Who took you as his wife?
Or the kids you bore?
The things you saw?
The hard times you were made to endure?
What's your story?
What's your story,
 Alyandabu?

Drought

She stared across the treeless plain
That often had enthralled
Today the five year drought still burned
The tortured sight appalled.
Their barren, shelly cattle
Stood dying on their feet
She watched her husband riding home
A spectre in defeat.

The message came that morning
On the big bank's letterhead
With trembling hand she opened it
And this is what it said:
"The auction of your property
Will go ahead as planned
Three weeks from now, walk in, walk out,
Arrangements are in hand".

It was too much for the woman
She cursed the drought, and then
She shouted out," I can't see how
It's ever gonna rain again".

She thought of love and passion
In the big old bed where they
Had made the sons and daughters
Who'd now all gone away.
She held her husband tenderly
Their calloused hands clamped tight
They stared into the darkness
Of never-ending night.

She took her husband's shotgun
That she found behind the door
She'd seen that desperate, haunted look
On her father's face before
She quietly packed her linen,
The photos and the gun
The ribbons and the trophies
Their little kids had won.

It was too much for the woman etc

The auctioneer was at his best
He jollied up the throng
A city lawyer bought the place
He got it for a song.
This handy bush investment
Would pay his income tax
Fly friends in for the weekend
A great place to relax.

It was too much for the woman etc.

Lum Loy of Darwin: everyone called her Granny
By permission of Jeanette Cook

CHAPTER 16

Multi-Cultural Australia: Are You Fair Dinkum?

> Watch her walking down Cavenagh Street
> Silk pyjamas, slippered feet,
> Everyone just called her Granny.
>
> Ted Egan, *Granny*

Aboriginals would be entitled to shake their heads at the proprietorial, xenophobic stance on immigration characteristic of Australia today. But the irony is that most First Australians agree with current immigration policies that decree 'boat people' claiming refugee status to be bad news. Maybe their own history helps Aboriginals frame that attitude. Perhaps they are aware that they usually remain at the end of the queue, regardless of who comes to live in Australia. New arrivals are reassured to find people below themselves on the pecking order. Invariably those people are the impecunious Aboriginals.

The first time Australians felt endangered by the arrival of migrants was during the Gold Rush days when many thousands of Chinese arrived to participate in the bonanza. The objection was on straight racial grounds. The alarmists described in lurid detail how the 'yellow hordes' would take over the country. Cartoonists had a field day, showing fanged, pitchfork-wielding Oriental monsters devouring babies, burning houses, smoking opium pipes, and advancing in savage mobs to conquer the country and threaten the lifestyle.

Anti-Chinese laws were passed. From 1857, various *Acts To Regulate The Presence of the Chinese Population in Victoria* prescribed heavy fees for entry by Chinese into Victoria, where most of the gold strikes occurred. The Chinese response was to take their ships to Robe, a port not far from the South

Australian Victorian border. The Chinese miners disembarked there in hundreds, and 'jig-jogged' through western Victoria to Ballarat and Bendigo. There, where thousands of men were now frantically digging and sluicing for the coveted gold, the disciplined Chinese made an immediate impact. They introduced ingenious techniques for obtaining gold, did not drink alcohol, and worked to strict strategies. The white diggers and authorities felt that here was a real threat to 'the Australian way of life' which was based on the 'she'll be right' philosophies that were, and are still, the rationalisation for a fairly lazy existence in a hard but bountiful land.

Fair Dinkum

If something is described as 'fair dinkum' in Australia, it means that it is *really* true. The expression is used both before and after a statement. What is not widely known is that 'fair dinkum' has a Chinese origin. When the Chinese diggers arrived on the Australian goldfields, they often used the words 'xing kim' meaning 'real gold', to distinguish the real precious metal from the worthless 'fool's gold' (pyrites) often presented for sale. The words became common parlance among all diggers and were eventually corrupted to 'ding kim', then 'dinkum'. Eventually, for whatever reason, 'fair dinkum' emerged.

And that's fair dinkum.

The Chinese never initiated violence, and there was plenty of gold on the Victorian diggings, where they came to be kept apart but were tolerated. There were sporadic bouts of pigtail-pulling, and other alcohol-inspired taunting of the Chinese diggers. At Lambing Flat, New South Wales, in 1861, anti-Chinese riots resulted in the murder of several Chinese. *The Bulletin*, a magazine destined to become 'The Bushman's Bible' and the voice of Australian nationalism, adopted as its slogan *Australia for the White Man*. That slogan was in place on page one, until the 1950s.

None of the supposed threats to the Australian lifestyle ever came to pass. The first Chinese immigrants were men only, who kept to themselves and worked hard at whatever occupation they chose. In earlier days they were obviously working to the instructions of entrepreneurs back in China. There are many tales about how the Chinese smuggled gold back to their masters. All dead bodies repatriated to their homeland were reputed to be stuffed with gold.

*From Melbourne in 1950 to Darwin in 2002:
the author with friend Ron Chin, grandson of Granny Lum Loy*
Photos: Ted Egan

Gradually the Chinese spread around the continent, and their presence was generally benign. They grew fruit and vegetables where nobody else could. They opened general stores and proved to be very fair traders. They opened laundries and tailoring shops, and cooked exotic meals - nothing like the roast meat and three vegetables that formed the staple Australian diet. And they worked as 'navvies' on railway construction and other projects. At this time the Australian population was rising steadily due to the influx of Caucasian people from all parts of the world, and the Chinese were a tiny minority. Yet politicians felt it necessary to institute what came to be known as the White Australia Policy. The *Immigration Restriction Act* formed part of new federal laws in 1901. Even in the 1950s politicians like Arthur Calwell, leader of the Australian Labor Party (ALP), felt quite comfortable reminding Australians that "two Wongs don't make a white".

The White Australia policy was brutal, simple. When a newcomer applied for residence in any part of Australia, the migration officials were empowered to submit the applicant to a dictation test in *any* European language. Fail, and you're on your bike. Did anybody mention race?

> ## The Children of Billy Hughes
>
> During the Gallipoli Campaign in World War I a group of Maltese men were employed as labourers by the Australian Forces. Under heavy fire at most times, the Maltese carried out all sorts of menial tasks. When Gallipoli was evacuated in December 1915, British officials wondered what to do with the Maltese. They could not send them home for Malta was occupied by the Germans, so it was decided that they should go to Australia. They were shipped to Fremantle, arriving in 1916 just as the arguments around the Conscription Referendum, initiated by pro-conscriptionist Prime Minister W M (Billy) Hughes, were at their most heated. Anti-conscriptionists argued that, if all Australian men were sent overseas to the war the 'dark hordes' would invade Australia, rape the women and take the jobs. So the olive-skinned Maltese unwittingly created mayhem. Under the White Australia policy, it was easy to keep them out when they failed the famous dictation test in Dutch. For the next three years their ship cruised the Pacific. The Maltese were turned back by every country they visited. It was not until 1919 that their heroism at Gallipoli was recognised and they were welcomed as citizens of Australia. To this day they are known among Australian Maltese as 'it'tfal ta Billy Hughes' - the children of Billy Hughes.

Although today the White Australia policy is long since gone, and Australia is one of the most racially and culturally diversified countries in the world, there remains an Anglo Saxon and Celtic majority. For many of these xenophobia is very real.

And other long term Australians from different racial or cultural backgrounds have been quick to take on the same conservatism. The threat of the yellow hordes now has a religious element too; fierce debate now rages about the 'Islamic invasion', as the latest threat to the Australian lifestyle.

The example set by the Chinese in Darwin, the capital of Australia's Northern Territory, shows that in these matters patience and sufficient tolerance bring admirable integration, and an enrichment of the nation. The Chinese came as 'coolies' to build the North Australian Railway in the 1870s. During excavation for the railway, gold was discovered. The Chinese were on the spot, as miners, storekeepers and general labourers. They stayed and integrated. In the 1950s the most popular name in the Darwin phonebook was not Smith but Chin. Many generations later they are marvellous citizens of Australia, as 'ocker' as Paul Hogan in their Australian-ness, and leaders in commerce, the professions, sport and cultural life. In Darwin, the Joss House remains - but gentrified - and today is called the Temple. They still speak their own Chinese language when it suits them.

Everyone calls her Granny

Granny Lum Loy was known as Lee Mu when she arrived in Darwin from China in the 1880s, aged seven. She was reared by relations on the North Australian goldfields, and when she married she went to Emungalin (Katherine) with her husband. She was a renowned horticulturist, growing mangoes, bananas, pineapples and other tropical fruits to sell to the locals. In later years she was a prominent figure in Darwin as she walked the streets, selling fruit, vegetables, eggs and 'salty plums' from huge baskets carried on a bamboo pole. The tiny little lady was much-loved, and everybody called her Granny. When she died at 97, she had children, grandchildren and great grandchildren as some of the leading citizens of Darwin. Her funeral was one of the largest ever in the town. The procession took several hours as the hearse visited Granny's many garden sites around Darwin.

Granny

She was a sprightly little Cricket
The thickness of a stick, it seemed
She never ever stopped
Scurried daily into Darwin
Where all the people knew her,
Everybody loved her,
Everyone just called her Granny.

Watch her walking down Cavenagh Street
Silk pyjamas, slippered feet,
Selling mangoes, vegies, eggs
And she'll run you off your legs
That's the way it is with Granny.

She was the cutest little Butterfly
Every day as she passed by,
I'd wave and call : "Ne ho ma?"
She'd "Ho Ho" her reply.
The oldest Darwin people
Said when they were young children,
Even then they'd call her Granny.

Watch her walking down Cavenagh Street
Silk pyjamas, slippered feet,
Watch her go, every day,
To the Joss House, time to pray,
That's the way it is with Granny.

She was a funny little Kitten
Hard work had made her fit, and
She'd come down to Australia
From China as a child.
She lived to ninety-seven
Surrounded by her family
And every one just called her Granny.

Watch her walking down Cavenagh Street
Silk pyjamas, slippered feet,
Bamboo pole, baskets full,
Waving to the kids at school
That's the way it is with Granny.

And when Granny died in Darwin
We took her for a ride
To every place she'd lived
In her long and active life.
The Darwin traffic halted
The policemen all saluted
And everybody waved to Granny.

Watch her driving down Cavenagh Street
Silk pyjamas, slippered feet
Sue Wah Chin, Albert Chan,
Henry Lee, White Chinaman
Everybody waved to Granny.

Hai gen kwi hang do
Hong yen gai
Jak ing gow xu
Sam tor hai

Queenie Chin, Old Chin Gong
Lorna Lim and Alex Fong,
Mary Chan, Yot Cheong Loong
There's her grandson, Chin Xu Hoong
Gor gor doo ham sang ah Lui Por
Everybody waved to Granny.

Bush Woman

She's living on a station
In an outback situation
And the first things that you notice
Are the lines on her tanned face
But those wrinkles frame the twinkles
That light her eyes with laughter
When she talks about her children
And the fact that she's their teacher
She says: "Isn't that amazing?
I myself had little schooling".
But she reckons it's her duty,
Give the kids an education,
For she'd never leave the station life
She's leading - with her husband,
Somewhere, in the outback, in the bush.

Fits the Correspondence lessons
In among the thousand other jobs
A woman in the the bush has to do, like
Bleed the generator, bake the bread, tend the chooks,
Late at night she 'does the books'.
Bottle feeds the little Joey
The kids had promised they'd look after,
Checks the baby, has a 'cuppa'
Then recalls she must be up at six
To go to town, to get the part
To make the grader start .
Turns her snoring husband on his better side
Says: "'Night-'night , Sexy,"
Then, wearily, she tumbles into bed.

She's about as soft as butter,
She's as gentle as a kitten,
She's as tough as rugged granite
She's as savage as a tiger,
If you jeopardise her children
You'd quickly wish you hadn't,
But she'll laugh and lead the singing at the ICPA party
And she'll make the ginger beer,
Bake a sponge, run the cake stall,
Nothing special, nothing flash
But nice to raise a little cash
Money for the Flying Doctor,
Never know, it might be your turn next
When you're living - in the bush.

And maybe once, or twice a year
Certainly her husband's birthday,
Organise a baby sitter, just the two of them for dinner
All dressed up, and looking gorgeous
On the second glass of bubbly
She gets just a little woozy
Looks into her husband's eyes,
Says: "Oh, I love you, really love you".
He says: "Shoosh!" But she can tell
He's feeling great, because as well as mate
He knows that she's his lover,
There could never be another
And they're sharing life together
Somewhere, in the outback, in the bush.

And she's the backbone of this country
She's alive and well today
She's the mainstay of Australia
And that's all there is to say.

*Striking gold: monument in Kalgoorlie honours
Paddy Hannan, gold pioneer*
By permission of the National Library of Australia

CHAPTER 17

Mining: Boom & Bust

> When first I left Old England's shore
> Such yarns as we were told
> Of how folks in Australia
> Could pick up lumps of gold
>
> (Anon.) *Old Bush Songs*, 1905

Mining in Australia began with the discovery of gold but it was increasing global industrialisation that brought attention to other rich mineral deposits all over the continent. The country's age, size and emptiness brought a realization that there were bound to be mineral riches under its dusty ground. And so it turned out. Both coking and steaming coal was in plentiful supply and spawned huge industrial complexes at Newcastle and Port Kembla in New South Wales. Railways were built to connect new coalfields in Queensland to the coastal ports. Huge brown coal fields were exploited in Victoria and South Australia. Chimneys belched smoke, power was generated, factories and steelworks were established, and exports swelled the nation's coffers.

Enormous silver, lead, zinc and copper fields were discovered at places as far apart as Mt Lyell on the inaccessible west coast of Tasmania, Broken Hill in New South Wales and Mount Isa in north-west Queensland. Gold continued to be the elusive mistress of many of the prospectors, but often in their quest for gold they found themselves opting instead to mine the many other minerals that were relatively easy to exploit. Roads and railways spread across the nation to link the miners with the farmers and pastoralists. Towns developed quickly in the most unlikely places. The pioneering spirit of Australia truly developed in the period between 1850 and Federation in 1901.

Digging up the Dirt

The raffish character Marsupial Joe depicted in the song of the same name is not apocryphal. He and his ilk were to be found in mining towns throughout Western Australia during the great mining boom of the 1970s.

But he also had his counterparts in Pitt Street and Collins Street, the financial districts of Sydney and Melbourne. The only difference between he and them was that they were dressed in suits, and quaffed squiff (Australian for champagne now that the French have banned the use of the word for any product fermented outside France)

It worked like this. A sharebroker would receive a tip from a geologist in a mining area that a survey team had discovered nickel or another valuable metal in a remote part of the desert. Very few of these 'tips' were genuine, and not a few originated in brokers' offices. Including some of the most respected brokers in town.

A lunch with a pliable journalist would ensure that the latter would return to his newsroom with the cry of 'Bosom's Creek has struck nickel', or something like that. Colleagues would pick up their phones and call their brokers to buy, the journalist and his lunch hosts would already have done so.

The next morning, post publication, the unsuspecting investing public would follow suit. Indeed, so great was the fervour for mining shares, that even those who doubted the validity of the story would buy. The perpetrators of the story, the precursors of the dot.com boomers of 1999, sold, and enjoyed their winnings.

It has to be said that the great Australian stock market mining boom was some years before world stock markets took insider trading seriously, punishable by years in jail. Insider trading was the way markets worked. Ramping - talking up a stock while simultaneously selling it - was also a normality.

But this was something else. Millions of dollars were made on the strength of a report of a mining 'find' which, when the geologists' report arrived, turned out to be no more than an empty hole in the desert. Much of the activity happened 12,000 miles away from the geologist's hammers. In London investors followed like sheep, only to see their money vanish as star spangled stocks like Poseidon turned out to be not what the writers in the Sunday business pages had forecast. One London merchant banker told The Observer's business editor that it was the "Australians getting their own back on the Poms".

But the two year spurt and fall was to sully the Australian financial markets' reputation, which took years to restore. An inquiry by the Senate noted that investors' confidence had been "severely shaken". Many years later this report still makes fascinating reading.

One thoroughly dishonest practice described by the report told how some household name brokers bought very large blocks of shares in early trading on their own account - in other words for themselves. By lunchtime word would be out that a certain mining stock - quite often Poseidon - was on the move, and this would lead to heavy public buying. The broking house would then unload a substantial chunk of its purchases to the enthusiastic buyers. When the price inevitably fell back, the broker would unload any onsold stock on to those of its own clients that had given it discretion to buy and sell on their behalf. But these sales were, of course, made at the day's earlier peak prices, enabling the firm to make a profit out of its own clients. To add insult to injury the brokers then charged these clients commission.

The good news is that today much has changed, and the Australian Stock Exchange has a reputation that puts it in the highest league.

Even the Cinderella State, Western Australia was to feature. When Arthur Bayley and William Ford found gold at Coolgardie in 1892 and Paddy Hannan followed up with a bonanza in 1893, the subsequent goldrushes established 'The Golden Mile' between Kalgoorlie and Coolgardie. Australia's biggest state, which had been teetering, almost bankrupt, suddenly started to develop its independent spirit. The Sandgropers dubbed their colony 'The Golden West' and showed the world how to operate gold mines in desert regions. The superb engineer, C Y O'Connor, not only ran a pipeline 450 miles from Perth to Kalgoorlie to make the desert bloom, but he also designed an innovative port at Fremantle to handle the shipping boom which followed. The Western Australians were able to demand a railway from the eastern states to Kalgoorlie as part of their agreement to Federation of the Australian States. Otherwise, they said, we'll secede, and rip the guts out of Australia. They still say it, when it suits them.

Old workings: abandoned copper mine at Mt. Lyall, Tasmania
© Wolfgang Sievers. By permission of the National Library of Australia

Since those days mining has been the biggest earner for the Australian economy. The major old mining towns are Ballarat and Bendigo (Vic) Broken Hill, Lithgow, Wollongong, Newcastle (NSW), Kalgoorlie (WA), Mt Isa, Mt Morgan, (Qld), Queenstown (Tas). In later years many smaller but prosperous and dynamic towns have been built in Western Australia for iron ore, gold and nickel, in Queensland for coal and bauxite, silver-lead and zinc, in the Northern Territory for manganese, bauxite and uranium, and in South Australia for coal, silver, lead, copper and uranium.

These are places where 'Jack and Jill' are as good as their masters, where town planning and architecture have set high standards and where cultural and sporting pursuits balance the strong work ethic. The combined influence of mining companies and trades unions has created admirable working conditions and, for the most part, benign community life. The mining towns are invariably remote, usually hot, but at the same time ideal for families. There are well-paid jobs for Mum and Dad, and fantastic conditions and amenities for the kids. There will always be industrial disputes and in the past there have been many acrimonious strikes but they are always resolved, for the value of the minerals prevails. In earlier times, care of the environment was a low priority but today tailings dams, green belts and emission controls have made the mining industry in Australia responsible. It is the industrial backbone of the nation.

Chance find of Rusty Mountain

Gold may have been the glamour metal, but the mineral that transformed Australia into the world's greatest quarry was iron ore. Yet the discovery of the of this strategic metal in large quantities was accidental, and at a time when the government believed the country had so little iron that it banned all exports of it.

It happened in November 1952 when Lang Hancock, a Western Australian grazier, was flying his Auster light plane in the mountainous Pilbara region of Western Australia, and found himself in thick low cloud. Fearing he might be lost and in danger, he decided to track the Turner river knowing it would eventually lead to the Indian Ocean.

Passing through a gorge, he noticed that the escarpment to his right appeared to be covered in rust. 'That must be iron', he thought.

Some weeks later he returned to the gorge and landed on an area of spinifex that had seldom, if ever, been visited by white men. Samples confirmed that the red-ochre coloured mountainside was indeed iron ore. Hancock headed to Perth to stake his claim to the mining rights to what turned out to be the largest deposits of the metal on earth.

But turning his discovery into a pile of cash that later made him Australia's richest man was not easy. Prime Minister Robert Menzies was adamant that iron would never be exported.

Hancock sought the help of the dynamic premier of Western Australia, Sir Charles Court, who was happy enough to put pressure on Canberra, but saw this newfound resource as a means of industrialising the state. Court saw the valued added benefits of exporting steel rather than iron ore.

By now Hancock had Japanese steel mills lined up to invest in his mining projects and buy the iron ore, but a licence was needed. "Promise to build a steel mill", Hancock urged them. It did the trick, and so mining began Ironically the steel mill was never built. Broken Hill Proprietary (BHP), Australia's biggest company, with steel manufacturing plants in Newcastle and Port Kembla, dominated the industry, and certainly did not want competition from an upstart in the west, owned in part by Japan Inc. BHP had a strong voice in Canberra, and that was that.

Marsupial Joe

It was way out west, a country town,
And old Prospector Joe
Rattled up the road in his battered old truck
From his outback mining show.
He breasted the bar, ordered a beer
Counted out his dough,
But the Publican said: "You're three cents short,
And I reckon you'll have to go".

Joe pulled a tobacco tin out of his kick
As he walked towards the door.
And he looked at the Publican in disgust -
Said: "Mate, you think I'm poor.
But inside this tin are 'samples', mate
And I am fairly sure,
I'll have no financial worries, mate,
From now to ever more".

With the incredible speed of insatiable greed
The Publican was heard to say
"Joe, old pal, old cobber, old friend,
I'd love to have you stay.
Have a few free drinks, and meals,
We'll send your 'samples' for assay
We'll form a mining company
This very blooming day".

Rumours spread like wild fire,
The locals filled the bar
They shouted Joe exotic drinks,
And he puffed on a big cigar.
The sheilas all proposed to him,
Folks came from near and far
They formed a mining company
And they called it Western Star.

Joe wouldn't let the locals see
The contents of his tin
But as he packed it carefully
He wore a crafty grin
Went down to the Post Office
Dropped his parcel in
And the Publican stuck as close to Joe
As a plaster on his shin.

They wined Joe, they dined Joe,
They drove him all around
New tyres and a clutch for his old red truck
To make it safe and sound.
For two full weeks old Joe was King
He never bought a round
But when the message came from The School of Mines
He was nowhere to be found.

They searched for Joe both high and low
But he'd flown off like a bird,
So the Publican grabbed Joe's telegram
And demanded to be heard.
He ripped it open, swallowed, gasped,
Then he spluttered out these words,
"Your samples are identified as top-grade kangaroo turds!"

*Proud Anzac: Australians attained nationhood after
the tragic defeat at Gallipoli*
Bronze by Wallace Anderson

CHAPTER 18

The Spirit Of ANZAC

> On the question of saluting, an Australian digger said to a pompous, monocled English officer: "As a matter of fact, mate, we've decided to cut that out completely".
>
> Ted Egan, *The Anzacs*

From the 'spirit of the bush' developed by the overlanders, the shearers, the drovers, the miners, the rail and road construction workers and the timber cutters and their families, came a rural nostalgia that is common to many Australians. The paradox is that from the start of white settlement in Australia the vast majority of its citizens have lived in towns and cities hugging the coastline. The big dream of Australians is embodied in an ocean view, but *The Complete Works* of Banjo Paterson and Henry Lawson are always on the bookshelves. The Namatjira watercolours are on the living room walls. You watch your beachfront real estate appreciate in value in the same proportions as you yearn to be like Clancy, droving on the western plains.

The bush spirit has enabled all Australians to have an *alter ego*, be it the Drover's Wife or the Man from Snowy River. "I'd have done the same sorts of things", people reassure themselves. It is a fine spur to a nation that has always prided itself on its achievements, sympathy for the underdog, tolerance, and friendliness. The xenophobia is still there but less so, for the White Australia Policy is *de jure* and almost *de facto* dead and buried. There is conservatism but Australia does not suffer from hard-headed, institutionalised racism based on religious dogma. Not yet.

The bush heroes are good role models. The Bush Woman,

in the poem of the same name, is typical of hundreds of thousands of women who have been real pioneers in the toughest and most demanding of situations throughout frontier Australia. These women are very real. They are alive and well today. They have reared children in sometimes impossible situations, they have been teachers and nurses to those children. They have fought fires, battled floods and taken on the banks when in financial crisis, sharing all sorts of hardships with their husbands and partners. They always find time for a laugh, a chat with the girls (and the blokes), and the pursuit of cultural interests. Still operating on a frontier, today's women are pilots, truck drivers, mechanics, bulldozer operators, doctors, teachers, nurses, computer 'magicians', photographers, sculptors and musicians. As fundraisers they are the backbone of those admirable frontier organisations like CWA, ICPA, RFDS, and VISE. And above all, they are the mothers of the nation.

Many bush-loving Australians also have a quite remarkable residual affinity with the United Kingdom. In the 1999 Referendum on whether Australia should become a Republic, the majority of voters opted for a retention of the monarchy. Incongruously and to the bafflement of most international observers, the voters opted to keep the Queen of England as Queen of Australia. There is still something of a 'colonial cringe' in Australia, although most Australians would deny it.

During the Boer War and indeed during several previous British skirmishes in Africa, young Australians hastened to enlist to fight as loyal members of the British Empire for Queen and Country. Curiously, at the same time in Australia there were determined efforts to promote a republic, and British migrants were lampooned as stupid, class-ridden 'Pommies' (Products of Mother England). Even when Harry 'Breaker' Morant and Peter Handcock were executed at Pretoria Gaol on 27 February 1902, as scapegoats to cover for the blunders of British commanders in South Africa, it did not diminish the love of Empire instilled in Australians. When General Kitchener, who had insisted on the scalps of Morant and Handcock, visited Australia in 1910, he was hailed as the conquering hero. Military units and school Cadet Corps were established on a compulsory level, just in case the Empire might issue a call-to-arms.

It was not long coming. In 1914, when Britain declared war on Germany, that declaration immediately incorporated Australia and the other dominions. Australian men flocked to the drill halls, established post-Kitchener, to sign up as volunteers. The most stringent fitness standards were set and the cream of Australia's men signed on at 'six bob a day' (six shillings, or 30p in current money). The studio photographs were taken, and didn't they look superb in their rough khaki uniforms, the leggings, the feathers, the spurs, the whips under the arm? The prime choice was to enrol in the Light Horse Regiments, for were we not the greatest horsemen in the world? The Man from Snowy River was about to ride again. A couple of cavalry charges across Europe, and we'll rout the Hun, and be home for Christmas. Little did they know.

The immortal word ANZAC was coined at Albany in Western Australia, in November 1914. The amalgamation of the Australian and New Zealand Army Corps preceded their departure in troopships, bound for England, and thence the Western Front.

But why did Australians enlist? As volunteers? The questions were asked time and time again. The soldiers were bemused. "It seemed like a good idea. We just felt, well, we just felt we had a duty to the Empire". Men who had fought battles over working conditions at Barcaldine and, during the 1890s, long maritime strikes, were happy to enlist to serve under commanding officers like General Chauvel, a hated and noted strike-breaker, and to fight a sordid war contrived by European states to take attention away from the great social problems of the time. It was a war that would bring the greatest slaughter of all time. A war so awful that it came to be called 'the war to end all wars'. A war that should never have been waged.

For most of the recruits it was a great opportunity for adventure, the chance-of-a-lifetime to visit 'Home' or the 'Mother Country', as England was fondly dubbed by Australians in 1914, and indeed until the 1950s. The colonial troops were all British Subjects yearning to be 'blooded' in war. Those men not enlisting were goaded with white feathers by strident 'hags', encouraged for the most part by clergy and politicians, who themselves pledged 'the last man and the last

Cairo 1914: the Anzacs arrive in Egypt
By permission of the Australian War Memorial

shilling' as they stayed at home, played their war games and mouthed their smarmy rhetoric.

When the Anzac troopships reached Colombo they were given the unpalatable news that they would not be going to England but to Egypt. Turkey had entered the war on Germany's side, and Britain had vague plans for a southern offensive. On disembarkation in Egypt the Anzacs showed that they were going to be 'tough nuts' for the English commanders appointed to take control of the raw recruits for the combined Empire forces. Discipline was a dirty word to the wild colonial boys. Yes, the Australians would salute, but only railway porters. Certainly not salute the British officers, with their monocles and their 'toffy' voices. They were considered by the Anzacs to be pompous objects of ridicule. "These colonials need more polish and less spit", fumed a taunted British officer. The Anzacs marauded the shops, bazaars and brothels in Cairo. They stole donkeys and camels, and staged race meetings. They incorporated their versions of 'Gyppo' words into their version of the English language and they sang ribald songs.

> Queen Farida, gibbit backsheesh
> Queen Farida, gibbit backsheesh
> She's the Queen of all the wogs,
> The jackals and the dogs
> Inta kwais, kwais katir, bungaree, bardi.

Whatever that meant.

But then the fun was over and it was time to fight. They went first to Gallipoli, a point of entry into The Black Sea where, at dawn on 25 April 1915, they confronted 'Johnny Turk', as the Anzacs dubbed their redoubtable enemies, the Turks. That day is now deemed to be the day that Australia and New Zealand attained nationhood. It was the first 'blooding' of the two antipodaean outposts of Britain. The other Allied nations involved at the Dardanelles in 1915 - Great Britain, France, and India - all had experience of wars going back centuries, so for them the Gallipoli campaign is a distant, minor memory, even though their casualties were heavy.

In Turkey's case, the casualties were horrendous, and the Gallipoli campaign was the point at which Kemal Ataturk is deemed to have become the Father of the Turkish Republic. Turkey, Australia and New Zealand will forever observe 25 April as Anzac Day, first solemnly at dawn services, then with a march and ceremonies to remember the fallen, and finally a day of celebration for the birth of the nation.

Anzac Day is very revealing of the character of Australia and Australians, New Zealand and New Zealanders. The Allied Forces did not prevail against the Turks at Gallipoli; the Turks rightly insist that they were courageous winners in the fight to defend their homeland. What nation, other than Australia or New Zealand, would have as its most important day of remembrance, a public holiday to celebrate an honourable, if ignominious, defeat?

The Gallipoli campaign was six months of bloody trench and hand-to-hand fighting that achieved nothing but the slaughter of almost 140,000 young men, 87,000 of them Turks.

A feature of the campaign was the suicidal bayonet attacks constantly ordered by officers on both sides. On 19 May 1915, the day that Albert Jacka won Australia's first-ever Victoria Cross and the day a Turkish sniper killed both John Simpson and his donkey (see Chapter 19), 42,000 Turks stormed the Anzac trenches. They were butchered by coordinated and disciplined Australian firepower. Mangled bodies were sprawled in layers all over no-man's land. It was a crazy scenario. An eight-hour truce was declared, on 24 May 1915, to enable the living on both sides to bury the dead. Even more extraordinarily, Kemal Ataturk himself was escorted on horseback, blindfolded, into General William Birdwood's headquarters. The ensuing conference saw the adversaries trying to establish that it was not they who needed an armistice. As Alan Moorehead reports:

> "There were the Turkish *beys* in their gold lace, the British generals in their red tabs.... But the atmosphere was relieved briefly by an Australian soldier unaware of what was going on inside the dugout. He put his head around the canvas flap and demanded: 'Have any of you bastards got my kettle?'"

Going home: the Brits say farewell to the courageous Anzacs as they leave Southampton for home in 1919
By permission of the Australian War Memorial

In the trenches the white flags rose and the Anzacs and the Turks emerged like apprehensive rabbits, unsure of the safety of it all. Elaborate steps were taken to maintain the peace as they then undertook the grisly task of identifying and burying their dead. That accomplished, they exchanged pleasantries, souvenirs and cigarettes, and then prepared to kill one another in the cleared space. Madness was restored.

In August 1915, the Australians were sent into suicidal attempts to capture The Nek, the peak at the top of a narrow ridge of a cliff face. The plan was that heavy British artillery would cover the bayonet charge, in four waves each of 150 men, as they 'hopped the bags' and charged up a steep slope to the Turkish lines. For some reason - probably an error in the synchronization of watches - all shelling ceased, rather than started at the appointed 4.30 am, as though to alert the Turks that something was afoot. As the four lines of Australians were ordered to charge, the Turks cut them to pieces. None of the 600 Australians went further than ten metres.

Gallipoli was evacuated by the Allied Forces in November 1915. Today it is becoming *de rigeur* for young Australians to visit Gallipoli on Anzac Day. Though some Australians have established a reputation as ugly international tourists, it is redeemed somewhat by the sight of young Australians and Turks embracing, exchanging flowers and together mourning the futility of war. Will somebody please send that message to the politicians, the archbishops, and the mullahs? Tell them to stop teaching that wars are honourable or noble, or pulling out the old turnip that 'God is on our side'.

After Gallipoli, the Australians split into two groups. The Light Horse regiments and the Camel Corps went to Palestine in the Middle East. The artillery and infantry regiments went to the Western Front, to fight in France and Flanders.

If the Anzacs thought Gallipoli was carnage, the Western Front was indescribable. For the next three years the Australians, all volunteers, were put into the front lines in France and Belgium, often to the point of absolute expendability. They were blown away, gassed and maimed both mentally and physically. Post-war, back in Australia there would be no shortage of legless lift operators for the next 25 years. On a per capita basis,

Australia suffered the highest casualty rates of any country involved in a war 12,000 miles from their homeland; a war that should never have been fought in the first place.

In the Middle East, conditions were familiar to many of the Light Horsemen who had come from arid regions of Australia. They were to cover themselves with glory as they and their sturdy Waler horses were used in lightning raids to support the British artillery attacks in the quest to capture Jerusalem and then Damascus. The highlight of their performances was the capture of Beersheba, a crucial part of the Allied offensive, for without the waters of Beersheba they would have been forced to withdraw from hard-won territory. On 30 October 1917, 800 members of the 4th and 12th Australian Light Horse charged for three miles under heavy fire. They then jumped the German and Turkish trenches, overwhelmed the confused enemy in maniacal hand-to-hand fighting, and nonchalantly rolled their cigarettes and watered their horses as the British officers rushed to congratulate them. Seven hundred Turks and Germans were captured by the Australians; thousands surrendered to them. It was the greatest cavalry charge in history.

The Australian Light Horse cavalry seize Beersheba in 1917
By permission of the Australian War Memorial

It was also the turning point in the Middle East theatre of war. Gaza and Jerusalem fell reasonably easily and after bitter fighting in 1918 the Allied Forces, led by the Australian Light Horse, captured Damascus.

In 1919, after the end of the war, the Australian soldiers were given the heart-rending task of destroying their horses. Quarantine regulations ordained that the horses could not be returned to Australia. The officers would not condone the sale of horses to Arabs, who were considered to be too cruel to animals. So a mass culling was ordered.

Most Australian Light Horsemen had taken their own horses, 120,000 in all, to the war. Only one horse returned to Australia. The Anzac troopers reported that putting down their faithful companions was the worst thing they encountered. Indeed, most men could not bring themselves to shoot their own animals; it was generally agreed to shoot your mate's horse, and he shot yours. The great Australian songwriter, Eric Bogle, wrote his beautiful, poignant song *It's As If He Knows*, in 2003, as a searing tribute to both the men and the horses.

Lest we forget: Grace's brothers Martin, Bob and Jack, were casualties of war.
Photos: Ted Egan

The Anzacs

We are the Anzacs, and we're true blue,
We're from Australia and New Zealand, too,
From Down Under, and we're telling you.
We're boozers and we're skiters,
But we're bloody good fighters, too./
We might curse and swear
But we'll be right there
In the fighting we won't turn a hair,
When the whips are cracking, everywhere
You'll find the Anzacs.

We've got shearers, and drovers, too
We've got city swells, and lots of blokes named Blue
As horsemen, we're the world's best yet
Ned Kelly's our CO, and don't you forget.
Would we go AWL? Don't be absurd!
Discipline! Now there's a dirty word.
We'll shout: "Maa leesh" and "Gibbit back sheesh"
We are the Anzacs.

We'll take orders, but only from the King,
We will play Two Up, so come on form a ring.
Come on digger, just a friendly game,
It's 'Come in Spinner' and heads are right, again.
We will salute, but only railway porters,
Mothers lock up your flaming daughters,
Inter kwais, kwais katir, bungaree, bardi.
We are the Anzacs.

A Song For Grace

I was a girl of thirteen when my three brothers went to the war
Martin, Robert and Jack, and as I waved from the door
I thought: "Who in the world could have brothers as handsome as they?"
Three Australian Light Horsemen, I see their proud figures today.

Our parents were Irish, with no love for England at all,
But their sons were Australian, and each bravely answered the call,
In their turned-up slouch hats, and their feathers, and leggings, and spurs,
The Empire, as much as my mother, knew these sons were hers.

CHORUS
At the going down of the sun
And in the morning
We will remember them
Lest we forget.

The mailman brought cards from Colombo, and then from Port Said,
Here's a photo of Jack, in Egypt, his first camel ride,
Look at young Bobby, in London, here, crossing The Strand,
And Martin writes: "Mum and Dad, life in the army is grand".

The same mailman brought us the news about our darling Jack,
"Regret to inform you your son John will never come back,

He died of his wounds at Gallipoli, so brave was he
He's awarded the Military Medal posthumously".

And at the going down of the sun etc.

When the telegram came, my mother collapsed, and I had,
The terrible task of breaking the news to my Dad.
With our old draught-horse, Punch, my father was ploughing the land
I ran to the paddock, the telegram clutched in my hand.

The Irishman read it, said : "Thank you, now leave me alone,
Go on back to the house, help your mother, she's there on her own".
He called: "Stand up, Punch, we have to get on with this job".
But I saw his slumped shoulders, and I heard his heart-rending sob.

At the going down of the sun etc

Well, Robert was gassed, and he always had pains in his head
Martin was shell-shocked, and he'd have better off dead
And I? I'm just an old lady who watched them all go
But I am the one you should ask about war, for I know
That all of these years have gone by, and I know the grief yet
Yes, I will remember them - I can't forget.

Beersheba

The soldiers ate their breakfast
Bully beef and biscuits
They'd ridden for the last two days and nights
Their faithful horses ground their oats
Through bitted mouths in nosebags
Veterans of a hundred desert fights.

CHORUS
It's through the Sinai desert, boys
On the way to Gaza
Jerusalem is in our sights
But first we need Beersheba
The waters of Beersheba.

Australian guns were blazing
On the slopes of Tel el Saba
The British fought the action to the west
But the Turks and Germans grimly
Manned the ramparts of Beersheba
Determined to withstand another test

Come on! Come on infantry!
Hit 'em hard, artillery,
If this operation's to succeed
Beersheba must be captured
We must take the town by nightfall
Beersheba's water is our greatest need.

It's through the Sinai Desert, boys etc

The day dragged on, the fight was grim
Sunset just an hour away
Chauvel could see the only way to go
"We'll charge their bloody trenches
With the Fourth and Twelfth Light Horse
It's the only way to win this little show".
Mount up! Fourth and Twelfth Light Horse!
Fix bayonets for the charge
Say your prayers and wave your mates goodbye

For you must ride those three long miles
And take the Turkish trenches
Beersheba boys, you must do or die.

It's through the Sinai desert, boys etc.

Across the rocky plain they rode
A trot to form the line
A canter for another mile or more
Eight hundred wild colonial boys
Then thundered to a gallop
Riding as they'd never done before.

Shells are bursting round them
Sheets of flame and dust
Horses and their riders blown apart
Still they charged relentlessly
A mile ahead and they can see
The trenches where the fight will really start

Machine guns fired and rifles spat
Their message at the horses that
Began to jump the trenches one by one
Then the fighting's hand to hand
The enemy could not withstand
Cold steel, and then the fighting's done.

The canvas troughs are then unrolled
The horses slake their thirst
Girths are slackened by Beersheba's Gate
The tired Australian horseman
Strokes the neck of his old Waler,
"Well done, well bloody done, my dear old mate".

It's through the Sinai Desert, boys,
On the way to Gaza
Jerusalem is in our sights
For now we've won Beersheba
The waters of Beersheba.

*John Simpson: war hero who never fired a shot.
He and his donkey were killed while saving lives at Gallipoli*

Drawing by Mark Egan, 1981

CHAPTER 19

Greater Love Than This: The Man With The Donkey

> **Dear Mother,**
> ... If I had known I wasn't coming home to England, I would not have joined the Australian Army ...
>
> **John Kirkpatrick, 1914**

Human beings are predictably unpredictable. Just when one feels that the world is full of criminals and cheats, some human being will perform a wonderful, selfless deed so atypical that we gasp. We should take it for granted; we should "Love our neighbours as ourselves"; we should "Do unto others as we would have them do unto us". The indictment of our so-called civilised society is that many pay lip-service to such sentiments, but few really expect them to be put into practice.

Yet even those sentiments are not totally selfless, for there is a certain *quid pro quo* to them. "You scratch my back, I'll scratch yours". The truly selfless gesture is done anonymously, without coercion, with no anticipation of favours or rewards in return. The ultimate in selflessness must be to sacrifice one's own life to save another, without inflicting harm on any third party in the process. So it is fitting that John Simpson Kirkpatrick is the best-known symbol of the Anzacs. The paradox is that the Anzacs acquired a reputation as fighters of unsurpassed ferocity and initiative. This man, on the other hand, never fired a shot in the Great World War.

He joined the Australian Imperial Force as soon as war broke out, enlisting at Fremantle under the name of John Simpson, although his surname was Kirkpatrick. Assigned to the 3rd Field Ambulance Corps, he sailed with the first troopships, leaving Western Australia in November 1914. He was 22 years old, and had worked around Australia for the previous four years, on ships and in mines, carrying his swag.

A sobering thought for contemporary Australians is that in today's slang Simpson, arguably Australia's greatest hero, would have to be classified as a 'Pommy bastard'. He constantly referred to England as 'home' and wrote to his mother that if he had known the troopships were taking the troops to Egypt and not England, as was supposed to be the case, he would not have volunteered to join the Australian army. It is not beyond speculation that joining the army was to be the means of a free trip home.

John Kirkpatrick was born in County Durham, England, in July 1892. His letters to his mother and sister tell us that he was a loving son and brother. He was generous, always sending home 'a couple of quid'(£2). A school teacher's assessment of his letters would probably be: Level of Interest - High. Grammar - Poor. Spelling - Seven out of Ten. He was an animal-lover, always solicitous for the old dog he had left behind in England and taking on board the troopship a pet possum that he carried in his shirt. He found a little donkey in a cave at Gallipoli. The donkey would be handy for carrying injured soldiers. Simpson named him Murphy.

From the first Anzac Day, 25 April 1915, to the day of his death, 19 May 1915, Simpson was constantly under fire, walking into 'No Man's Land' with Murphy, tending the wounded, bringing casualties back to the relative safety of the medical-aid posts without any fuss. When told he need not take such risks by going so often into danger zones, Simpson replied noncholantly: "That's my worry".

On 19 May a Turkish sniper shot him dead and then shot Murphy. History had a hero and hardened soldiers sobbed in grief.

There is no evidence of him being prompted by any higher motive or being 'holier-than-thou'. It is known that he frequented the bars and cafes in Cairo. It is said that he was not averse to a 'blue' - a fight. There is nothing about him to suggest that he would become the greatest single hero of the war. He did

Diggers on the Western Front: Soldier pulling rope: "Come on digger, can't you help us get you out of here?" Digger in mud: "Well, I'll take me feet out of the bloody stirrups if you like."
Drawing by Mark Egan, 1981

it in less than a month. He is justifiably immortal.

Yet Simpson was surrounded by other men as brave. There are no poems or songs or statues to honour Lance Corporal G T Hill, another stretcher-bearer who died the same day as Simpson. Hill carried his patient to the dressing station, sat quietly in the waiting ranks for the doctor to attend his comrade, and died without mentioning that he himself was mortally wounded.

Simpson, like Hill, would not have wanted any fuss. Neither received any medals for bravery, for awards like the Victoria Cross are given for a specific deed of ultimate heroism. For the brave stretcher-bearers, it was their job of work to place their own lives on the line in order to save others. Both were buried among the other heroes at Gallipoli..

> They shall not grow old
> As we that are left grow old
> Age shall not weary them
> Nor the years condemn
> At the going down of the sun
> And in the morning
> We will remember them.
> Lest we forget.
>
> *The Ode* recited each day in Returned Services Clubs (RSL Clubs) in Australia.

Greater Love Than This

Jack Kirkpatrick was an English lad
And when war broke out he was fairly glad
He joined the AIF, but he used his middle name.
Jack Simpson reckoned he'd take a trip
Go back to England on the first troop ship
Like his Aussie mates, he thought war was a game.

But the Turks joined Germany in the war
And the British planned to even the score
Off to Egypt the Anzac boys were sent
No Western Front for the Aussies yet
No trip to England would Simpson get,
In Cairo they would train for the big event.

A member of the Third Field Ambulance Corps
He scrambled through the water on Gallipoli's shore
Found a little donkey sheltering in a cave.
He said: "I'll call you Murphy, mate,
You and me, we'll get on great,
There's hundreds of wounded diggers out there to save."

CHORUS

Just a month, in the life, of an ordinary young man
An unknown bloke who went off to the war,
But the whole world knows of Simpson
And his gallant little donkey
And their deeds will be remembered, ever more,
Their deeds will be remembered ever more

Through machine gun fire, the stench and smoke,
You'd hear the voice of this cheerful bloke,
"I'll help you, digger," you'd hear young Simpson call.
With his little mate Murphy he braved the shells
In the hell that was made at the Dardanelles
He carried his wounded comrades through it all.

He took out nothing but a Red Cross flag
A medical kit and a water bag,
He never fired a shot in the Great World War
In Shrapnel Gully he wore a track
As he shielded his mates on the donkey's back
Greater love than this was never shown before.

CHORUS
Just a month etc

But on the 19th day of May
A sniper blew their lives away,
It's Simpson first, another shot, and Murphy dies
Hardened soldiers sobbed in grief
The whole thing seemed beyond belief,
They'd seen a legend pass before their eyes.

Call it folly if you please,
But hundreds there should have won VCs
Simpson's just a symbol of them all
He never thought of himself as great
Just a bloke with a duty to a mate
In the service of his mates did Simpson fall.

CHORUS
Just a month etc

*Click go the shears, boy: Jacky Howe,
world champion shearer at Alice Downs*
By permission of Robert Ingpen

CHAPTER 20

We'll Shear The Union Way

> But for every one that's sentenced
> Ten thousand won't forget
> When they gaol a man for striking
> It's a rich man's country yet.
>
> Helen Palmer, Doreen Bridges, *Ballad of 1891*

The shearing industry has undoubtedly been the principal source of Australian folklore. Bearded folk-singers who have never laid hands on a sheep talk of their 'tallies' as easily as they switch on their 'tellies'. The shearing songs, the poems, and the writings of people like Henry Lawson in *The Bulletin* contribute to the Australian rural nostalgia. They conjure smells of tar and lanolin, the mateship of 'the sheds', the struggles against the squattocracy and authority generally. Australia's unofficial anthem *Waltzing Matilda*, embodies it all, for the suicidal swagman, Frenchy Hoffmeister, was a unionist shearer:

> Up jumped the swagman
> Sprang into the billabong
> "You'll never take me alive" said he
> And his ghost may be heard
> As you pass by the billabong
> "You'll come a Waltzing Matilda with me"

The principles of Unionism began to be discussed on the Australian goldfields in the 1850s where Chartists like the eloquent Welshman Thomas Humffray, exhorted the workers to "stand united, for divided we fall". Talk spread to the shearing sheds, for often miners would also do seasonal work like shearing. The sheds grew bigger and bigger. By 1860, thousands of shearers worked at 3000 large sheds, shearing millions of sheep in all parts of Australia. It was inevitable that around the campfires and 'on the road' better conditions for workers would be discussed.

> ### Who'll go a waltzing, Matilda ...
>
> The song Waltzing Matilda has no connection with waltzing, or any form of dancing. The term derives from an old German tradition whereby itinerant apprentices were said to go *auf der Walz* as they roamed around the country pursuing work, rolling along like a barrel, *a Walz*. Their belongings, including greatcoats, were rolled into a bundle and were depicted as a substitute for a warm girl at night, hence *Mathilde*. In the Australian adaptation to this nomadic tradition the itinerant swagmen, who walked the outback following seasonal occupations like shearing, carried a bedroll consisting of a canvas sheet into which were rolled blanket(s) spare clothes (if any) and other precious belongings. The Australian form of *auf der Walz* was said to embody 'freedom on the Wallaby' as a man could travel in the uninhibited fashion of Australia's marsupials, his possessions on his back in the form of his Matilda, his swag.

The main grievance of shearers was that the 'squatters', as large landholders were generally called, insisted they had the unilateral right to set shearing rates. In 1840 the rate set for shearers was one pound (£1 - then 20 shillings) per 100 sheep, but the rate fluctuated down to ten shillings (10/-) in 1845, up to thirteen shillings (13/-) in 1857, back to £1 in 1870, but then reduced to seventeen shillings and sixpence (17/6) in 1880. All at the whim of the squatters. The shearers noted that the prices of stores and foodstuffs that, in the absence of shops, they were required to purchase from the squatters, progressed steadily upwards during the same period.

The militant shearers had had enough. In 1886 shearers' representative David Temple enlisted the services of the redoubtable William Guthrie Spence, secretary of the Amalgamated Miners Association of Victoria, to start up the Amalgamated Shearers Union. A national chord was struck:

> Through the West like thunder
> Rang out the shearers call
> The sheds will be "shore union"
> Or they won't be shorn at all.

Such assembly and association was still against the law, under the heading of 'conspiracy', and the squatters sought to invoke the *Masters and Servants Acts*, and old laws like the *Irish Coercion Act*, long since repealed in Britain but still held to be legal in Australia. In defiance, trade union congresses were held. The Shearers Union enrolled 20,000 members who sought to use the weapon of the 'closed shop', whereby they refused to work with non-unionists, or 'scabs'. Solidarity was international. When London dockworkers went on strike in 1889 Australian unionists sent them £30,000 - an incredible sum of money in those depressed times. To this day that action is regarded as a world landmark in the history of the trade union movement.

Things came to a head in the 1890s in Australia. The country verged on civil war, as thousands of angry, hungry, and in many cases armed unionists took on the powerful squatters and officialdom. In September 1890 unionists sought to prevent the Jondaryon (a large Queensland sheep station) wool clip - which had symbolically been declared 'black' after non-union labour was used in shearing the wool - from being loaded at Circular Quay in Sydney. The Riot Act was read, and a brutal cavalry charge routed the unionists. The officer commanding the troops called for "Three Cheers for Her Majesty" and the pastoralists, who had themselves formed a Pastoralists Union - one law for the rich, one for the poor - insisted on prosecutions under the *Masters and Servants Act*.

Dissension quickly spread to Queensland. When the 1891 shearing season started the unionists failed to reach agreement with the squatters on the 'closed shop' principle. Two hundred

Short back and sides: today's shearers use a clever harness to relieve backstrain in this toughest of jobs
Photo: Hans Boessem

shearers set up the first strike camp at Clermont, followed by others at Sandy Creek, Capella and Barcaldine. Ten thousand shearers assembled. Some crops were set alight, some woolsheds burnt. It was after his part in the burning of the Dagworth woolshed in northwest Queensland that the 'swagman' of *Waltzing Matilda* fame, Frenchy Hoffmeister, committed suicide, but not by drowning, as Banjo Paterson's song implies. The remorseful shearer shot himself. Not quite the stuff of a good folk song, but tragic in itself.

The pastoralists and their friends in Government were quick to respond. A combined force of squatters and government officials was formed. Hundreds of armed military and police were sent by train to western Queensland, and hundreds more 'specials, young gentlemen' joined them. Union leaders were arrested, papers seized and hundreds of arrests were made. There were occasional skirmishes, but the wonder of it all is that civil war did not eventuate.

The shearers flew the blue and silver Eureka flag at Barcaldine, and the nationalist Henry Lawson was moved to write in his poem, *Freedom on the Wallaby*:

> So we must fly a rebel flag
> As others did before us
> And we must sing a rebel song
> And join in rebel chorus
> We'll make those tyrants feel the sting
> Of those that they would throttle
> They needn't say the fault is ours
> If blood should stain the wattle.

They were brave words and the spirit of the men in the camps was unbroken. But when 14 of their leaders were jailed at Rockhampton in May 1891 on charges of conspiracy, it was obvious that the shearers would not win. By June 1891 the unionists had pulled down the rebel flag. They had run out of funds and other resources. The capitalist forces had won a crushing victory against the strikers. In 1894 another strike was similarly put down.

But the workers did not give up: they simply changed course. Realising that political clout had enabled the pastoralists to bring in the forces of law and order, and create the rules for 'strike-breaking', officials like William Spence began to form parliamentary associations, and to press for the principle of 'one man, one vote'. The end result was the foundation of the Australian Labor Party at Barcaldine, under the historic Tree of Knowledge; the election of a Queensland State Labor Government, the first of its kind in the world; and the gradual establishment, after Federation, of the Arbitration System to provide an Award for Shearers. Today the Australian Workers Union, a formidable, conservative body, is still fiercely representative of shearers' interests. Shearing remains a crucial, inspiring industry in Australia. The songs are sung at the folk festivals, and, as Henry Lawson said:

Freedom's 'on the Wallaby'
She'll knock the tyrants silly
She's going to light another fire
She'll boil another billy.

Australian nationalism was conceived at Eureka in 1854, and born at Anzac Cove in April 1915, after the labour pains of 1891. At all three events the common man lost convincingly at the time, yet prevailed in the long run. All three events are revered in Australian folklore. They're a weird mob, Australians.

The Union Way

In the year 1840, our wage was a pound
For each hundred sheep that we shore
But then all the squatters decided that they would
Determine our rates ever more.
So by the year 1880, with our rates again cut
Back to seventeen and six for 'a ton'
Thousands of shearers began to unite
And the long, long fight had begun.

CHORUS
So three cheers for Dave Temple,
Hooray for Billy Spence
Up with the Union, we say,
We are the shearers,
We'll form the Strike Camps
We'll shear the Union Way, hey, hey, hey
We'll shear the Union Way.

The squatters declared, they were just not prepared
To talk with mere working chaps
So they brought in the army, enlisted the scabs
And of course they controlled 'the traps'
Our leaders were tried, and stuck into gaol
For conspiracy, riot and treason,
And old Justice Harding, and Ranking and Tozer
Said shearers would be 'open season'.

CHORUS

So three groans for Tozer
Boo! Hoo! To old Ranking
Down with the squatters, we say,
Down with Judge Harding, the cops and the scabs,
We'll shear the Union Way, hey, hey, hey
We'll shear the Union Way.

Jondaryon's wool was declared to be 'black'
And the big Nineties Strikes were on.
Barcaldine, Clermont, the Rockhampton Trials
And all of our leaders were gone.
In the short term they won
But it made us unite
And one thing is certain today,
From the year 1890, while sheep are still shorn
We'll shear them the Union Way, hey, hey, hey
We'll shear the Union Way.

CHORUS

So three cheers for Jack Howe
Hooray for Billy Lane
Up with the Union we say
Down with the squatters
We are the shearers
We shear the Union Way, hey, hey, hey
We shear the Union Way

Don Bradman at practice: preparing to hit the English bowlers for six.
Hood Collection Mitchell Library, State Library of New South Wales

CHAPTER 21

The Tiger & The Don

> " Our Don Bradman,
> Well, I ask you, is he any good? "
>
> Jack O'Hagan

Don Bradman was once asked to select the greatest ever cricket team. Only slightly tongue-in-cheek the great batsman said: "O'Reilly, me, and any nine others!" After his death, it was revealed from his memoirs that 'The Don' had in fact selected himself and the great Australian bowler, Bill (Tiger) O'Reilly in his 'world best-ever' team, plus nine other champions, a majority of them Australians. And why not?

At the end of the 20th century, culminating in the 2000 Sydney Olympics, Australia could justifiably lay claim to be the best all-round sporting nation in the world. In world team sports - cricket (men and women), Rugby Union, Rugby League, Davis Cup tennis, women's field hockey, women's water polo and women's netball, Australia was reigning world champion, with an impressive long-term record in all of those sports. In other major team sports like basketball, rowing, soccer, and baseball, Australia continues to advance its world status.

There are Australian champions of world class in individual sports like swimming, golf, cycling, triathlon, surfing, snooker, squash, shooting, archery, even darts and skiing. In combined sports like horse racing, sailing, harness racing, motor sports, equestrian events including camp-drafting and rodeo, Australians are always in the top echelon.

At the 2000 Olympics Australia (population 20 million) finished fourth in the overall medal tally behind the United States (276 million), Russia (146 million), and China (1.3 billion). Australia won a total of 58 medals, of which 16 were gold.

And then there is the spectacular all-Australian football game called Aussie Rules or 'Footy', the most commercial game in Australia, but only played in the country of its origin. Name the sport and Australians will 'give it a go'.

Why is this? It is a combination of many things, but factors favourable to Australia are climate, space, economics, lifestyle, the stimulus of success in all sports and at all levels, and the ethnic make-up of the population. There is one other important ingredient.

Crucial to Australia's success in world team sports is the 'mateship' factor. On the goldfields, in the bush, in war and in sport, is the notion that a person, whether man or woman, needs to have mates on whom to rely. In return, your mates may depend entirely on you. For Australians, mateship is a must. It is Australia's greatest attribute.

Australia's land mass is equal to the United States (minus Alaska), ten times the size of the United Kingdom, and 20 times the size of Japan. The climate overall is temperate, but with snowfields for winter sports, a variety of ocean conditions for sailing, and warm to hot areas for the winter training of swimmers and athletes. Australian children grow up in a climate conducive to sport and exercise, where there is plenty of space and where sport is encouraged to an almost fanatical degree. There are usually first-class facilities and good coaches to allow any unusual talent to be recognised and fostered.

The ethnic composition of non-Aboriginal Australians up to the 1950s was predominantly Anglo Saxon and Celtic. With a good diet and temperate climate, and in a society where hard physical work was the norm for most people, over 150 years these Australians have grown bigger and stronger than their ancestors. The competitive attitudes of people from Britain and Ireland towards one another and, on an international level, towards the rest of the world, made Australians fearsome competitors. Increasingly good working conditions, and the balance of work and leisure enabled by the 40 hour working week, produced fit people for whom work was simply the means to enjoy leisure.

On any weekend in Australia that is evident. People are up and about at crazy hours to participate in organised sport and recreation, and they have the means to do so. There is an abundance of sports fields, swimming pools, acres of netball and tennis courts, gymnasiums, golf courses, beaches and marinas. Adults are catered for at every level, but the introduction of children to sport takes the form of tribal initiation. Children have the best uniforms and sporting tackle; there are coaches to remedy their every shortcoming and to teach them skills. Medical centres cater for every need and treat the slightest injuries. Parents are required to spend hours at weekends transporting children to sporting fixtures.

There are often ugly scenes when parents seeking to expunge their own inadequacies urge their children on to heights they never attained themselves. One of the greatest problems for sporting administrators in Australia is the behaviour of belligerent parents and other onlookers at children's sports. Children are not served well by their role-models in the popular sports, especially cricket and football, for many so-called elite players at top levels are often guilty of deplorable exhibitions of thuggery in the four football codes, and the new and quite disgraceful practice among cricketers called 'sledging'.

Since the 1970s Australia has been the worst cricketing nation in the world at this haranguing of opponents, on racial or indeed any grounds, and all Australian captains since Ian Chappell have much to answer for. Chappell, in his own defence, says that 'sledging' has always been there, it is only since cricket was so extensively televised that it has been recognised. He is wrong. It was not there previously. He and his (very good) teams started it in the 1970s, and Australians continue to be the worst offenders.

Although clearly the dominant nation in both forms of men's international cricket, since the 1970s Australia has established a record of being an exuberant, sometimes arrogant winner, but a petulant loser. The aggressive Australian media is as much to blame as the players themselves. It is a pity, for the general standard of Australia's representative cricketers can only be described as magnificent, largely due to the calibre of those same captains who allow or condone 'sledging'. But away with it. The game's the thing. Let the impeccable Richie Benaud be the role model for Australian cricket and cricketers. He was

Australia's best-ever captain. It was Benaud, almost single-handed, who reinvigorated cricket in the 1960s, after the English, led by Trevor Bailey, tried to kill it. With their stodgy batting, negative bowling and defensive field placements, English teams reduced Test matches to the farcical level where 150 runs per day was the norm. Along came Benaud, aided by Frank Worrell and the West Indians, and the great game survived.

Source of pride for Aboriginals:
'Golden Girl' and Wimbledon champion Evonne Goolagong
Photo: Herald and Weekly Times Ltd

By contrast, Australia has been particularly fortunate in the sport of tennis, through the admirable behaviour of earlier stars like John Bromwich, Harry Hopman and Adrian Quist in the halcyon tennis days before World War II. After the war Australia dominated world tennis for decades with wonderful players like Frank Sedgman, Ken McGregor, Ken Rosewall, Lew Hoad, Rod Laver, Roy Emerson, John Newcombe and a dozen others. In women's tennis there was Margaret Court and Evonne Goolagong. What marvellous players they all were. And what good sports! If they won they were modest: on the rare occasions when they lost they were fulsome in praise of their opponents. Present times are leaner for Australia, but let us hope that the Lleyton Hewitts copy the Rod Lavers of the world. Spare us, O Lord, from the monstrous brats like Jimmy Connors and John McEnroe.

In adolescence and right through adult life, talented athletes in Australia undergo intensive training at various institutes, academies and colleges. Scholarships at top schools enable any athlete of better-than-average talent to acquire some sort of certification that will justify use of the term 'tertiary education'.

At the elite level, astronomical sums are paid to athletes through sponsorship, endorsement, and share of television and other royalties. Top-flight golfers, tennis players, cricketers, footballers, swimmers and boxers receive millions of dollars a year through performances and endorsements. They travel first class, and stay at luxury hotels. Their every comment, slightest injury, every social move is reported *ad nauseam* on page one of every newspaper, and they headline TV and radio news.

In pre-television times sport was established as the means whereby people, particularly the working-class, organised their social life in Australia. "We make our own entertainment", people loved to say. Lawn bowls and fishing are the top sports in participatory terms. Golf is popular, and the standard of golf courses in the smallest of country towns always amazes international visitors. Tennis, cricket, football and netball tournaments for every age group from toddlers to seniors dominate social life, and are still a commendable feature of country towns and of every city suburb at weekends throughout the year. Highly organised inter-school tournaments are part of the curriculum of every school and college, sometimes to a dominant level. The many echelons of intense domestic competition ensure that there are always youngsters looking to follow the stars to the top level.

Above all other achievers, sporting heroes are idolised. Although Australia has had more than its share of success in the arts, science and business, it is invariably the sporting star who gets most media attention. The nation went into deep mourning when Don Bradman died. Adulation is not just for the human achievers. Racehorses are revered like gods. Suggest a list of Australian icons and Phar Lap will probably be listed somewhere near Dawn Fraser. Seek the name of the premier of one of the Australian state governments and most people outside that state will not know his or her name. But every Australian knows what horse won the Melbourne Cup. The entire nation stops for that famous race, and billions of dollars are gambled by people who hardly know which end of a horse kicks.

Australian track and field athletes and swimmers have been admirable ambassadors for their country and its lifestyle. Among the men, Herb Elliot stands supreme: never beaten at 1,500 metres, he was a true champion who also became a great sports administrator.

But the women! The 'golden girls' of past eras carried the Olympic torch for the last lap at the Sydney Olympic Stadium in 2000. They included Shirley Strickland, Marjorie Jackson, Dawn Fraser, Marlene Matthews, Betty Cuthbert (alas, in a wheelchair, but still gorgeous and smiling) Shane Gould, Raelene Boyle, Debbie Flintoff-King and Glynis Nunn - all superstars in their day; Gold Medal winners, and superb role models for young girls of any era. They finally passed the torch to Cathy Freeman, at that point not yet a Gold medallist but soon to become one. Freeman is perhaps the greatest role model of them all, in that she is the star now followed by so many young First Australian athletes of the future.

Australia is fortunate to have produced exemplary female athletes like Belinda Green and Zoe Goss as cricketers, Jan Stephenson and Karrie Webb in golf, Alyson Annan and Nova Peris, both Olympic hockey champions and Michelle Timms and Lauren Jackson as international basketballers. But they are just a selection. Every member of the Australian netball, softball and water polo teams combine continually to blitz all opposition.

More than equals in sport, music and the arts:
Aboriginal film star David Gulpilil
Photo: Aleck Jackomos, Australian Institute of Aboriginal Studies

The women swimmers, going back to the legendary Fannie Durack, surging through to Dawn Fraser, Lorraine Crapp, Tracy Wickham, Shane Gould, and on to Susie O'Neill, were always a delight. They were magnificent competitors who showed today's mermaids what constitutes a real champion. Among the Australian male swimmers, who will ever forget Murray Rose, Kieren Perkins, Ian Thorpe and Grant Hackett?

In men's cricket Don Bradman and Bill O'Reilly are surely the two greatest cricketers ever, joined by post-war champions like Keith Miller, Ray Lindwall, and Richie Benaud, through to today's great role models, Adam Gilchrist, Michael Bevan, Andy Bichel and Brett Lee. International footballers like John Eales,

Reg Gasnier and Harry Kewell; golfers like Peter Thompson and Greg Norman; cyclists like Hubert (Oppy) Opperman, Russell Mockridge and Sid Patterson; motor sports gems Jack Brabham, Wayne Gardiner, and Micky Doohan; jockeys like Scobie Breasley, Neville Sellwood and Damien Oliver; all were aggressive winners, tenacious losers, but always gracious performers.

The world game of football is always called soccer in Australia. That is because the two rugby codes, League and Union, and the home-grown Australian Rules are called football, or, to use a typical Australian abbreviation, 'footy'. Soccer is very popular, particularly among children, teachers and parents, for it is a unisex game that can easily be organised on the smallest of pitches, in the barest of school playgrounds, and with the least likelihood of injury.

In the past the problem for soccer in Australia was its image as a game played only by 'new chums' (from the United Kingdom) or 'wogs' (Europeans and other non-English speakers). Resistance has been fostered by the fact that teams have taken old world animosities onto the sporting arena. That is frowned on by most Australians. Games between Serbs and Croats, Italians and English, Greeks and Macedonians, can turn into bloodbaths, with spectators waving foreign flags and still intent on settling ancient, non-Australian conflicts. Officials are strenuous in their efforts to eliminate obvious European connections, and they pray for the time when Australian representation in the World Cup will win more hearts and minds to the game. On an individual level, Australian players are making a good, sometimes great impression with overseas teams.

Some consider it a shame that rugby followers in Australia are divided into the two games, Rugby Union and Rugby League. Imagine the calibre of a team combining the talents of League greats like Arthur Beetson, Clive Churchill, 'Changa' Langlands, Reg Gasnier, Johnny Raper, Wally Lewis, Mal Meninga, Paul Harragon and Andrew Johns with Union stars like Trevor Allen, Ken Catchpole, Mark Ella, Jules Guerasimoff, Tim Horan, David Campese, Matt Burke and John Eales. Add the many like Ken Thornett, Ray Price and Ricky Stuart, who played both codes at international level with such distinction?

The names don't equal a team, but you could build an invincible combination around any individual. Perhaps it is better that there are two codes; otherwise it would not be fair to the rest of the world.

Rugby Union has never been stronger in Australia, and the World Cup dominance has been accompanied by shrewd administration that has taken the former true-blue amateurs into the highest peaks of professionalism.

Sleight of hand: Mark Ella, one of the all-time greats of World Rugby Union and Australian captain
Photo: Herald and Weekly Times Ltd.

Rugby League stages almighty conflicts each year called State of Origin, whereby New South Wales (the 'Cockroaches') take on Queensland (the 'Cane Toads') - it's that sort of competition - in bloodthirsty confrontation that make the battle of Waterloo look like a garden party. Apart from that highlight, Rugby League battles to convince itself and the world that it is really an international game, but because of the dominance of Australia, World Cups are about as pointless as the selection of an 'All-Australian' Aussie Rules team. So where is the opposition?

Australian Rules football has produced many champions whose example to young players is as important as their huge talent. Take Leigh Matthews, Graham 'Polly' Farmer, Gavin Wanganeen, James Hird and Michael Voss, and you perhaps have the best five players ever in the great Australian game. They played hard, they loved to win, but if they lost, they copped it. Any young boy would do well to study every move of their illustrious careers.

It is a great pity that Australian Rules football in its present form will never become an international sport. It is much too complicated. It is impossible for strangers to follow the spectacle on a rectangular television screen, as the game is played with an oval ball on an oval-shaped pitch. There are too many (18) players per team, too many officials (umpires, runners, trainers, water-carriers) on the playing field. Soon they will need policemen to direct the traffic. There are too many inexplicable rules, and too much posing by players and officials alike, in the awareness that they are on television. It is called 'aerial ping pong' or 'cross country ballet' by its critics.

And yet the game combines spectacular features unmatched by any other sport in the world. Although Aussie Rules can be much better appreciated if watched 'live', the arrogance, parochialism and ignorance of the game's administrators has, to date, prevented effective demonstrations in other countries. There is a belief that an end-of-season match in London or Los Angeles between two Australian club teams will cause locals to feel privileged, to drop everything and flock to see the Australian supermen play the game that only Australians can play. What usually ensues is that the players behave like louts, and the spectators, mainly expatriate

Australians, use the day as the big opportunity to show Australian characteristics at their drunken, vomiting, brawling worst. Hybrid games seeking to combine the best features of Australian Rules and Gaelic (Irish) football produce a boring compromise that does little justice to either fine game.

Despite this, the AFL provides one of the best competitions of any sport in the world. The game is played at a skilful, relentless pace, with intimidating physical clashes, spectacular marking (catching the ball), colossal kicking and beautiful ball handling. Followers of the game speak of little else. The devotion of fans to their particular clubs does not border on fanaticism, it is fanaticism. Crowds are huge. Media coverage is relentless. The levels of skill and the physical fitness of the players must be seen to be believed. The rest of the world is really missing something. But that is a problem for the administrators of the game. Instead of trying to take London or Los Angeles by storm with the so-called superstars, they might be better advised to take a couple of school teams, involving a good racial 'fruit salad' of players, and tour Third World countries. It beats war.

In recent times Australia's Aboriginals have shown that with the same levels of encouragement given to other Australians they are more than just competitive: they are elite in their chosen sports. They excel at boxing and the various football codes, and are now being given opportunities in sports previously denied them. Tennis star Evonne Goolagong Cawley remains one of the world's great sporting icons, generations after her two Wimbledon titles. Cathy Freeman will forever be the most important symbol of the 2000 Olympics. She lit the Olympic Flame and later decimated the opposition with her scorching 400 metre run. Nova Peris won Olympic and Commonwealth gold medals for hockey and track. Wendell Sailor represented Australia at both Rugby League and Union. Patrick Johnson is a blistering, world-class sprinter. Michael Long's formidable career at Australian Rules Football has taken him to a full-time job spotting and fostering young Aboriginal athletes.

Past sporting eras were sad times for First Australians. Even if allowed to participate, Aboriginal athletes were invariably victims of discrimination, exploitation and prejudice. In the 1930s Ron Richards was probably as good, pound for pound, as any boxer ever in the world. Like dozens of other talented Aboriginal boxers Richards was manipulated by greedy managers to the point where he finished up shuffling, punch-drunk, around the Sydney Markets, checking the rubbish tins

He's a knockout: World Bantamweight champion Lionel Rose.
Photo: Herald and Weekly Times Ltd.

for scraps. He was often the victim of thuggish attacks by morons who would boast: "I flattened Ron Richards".

> He shuffled through the Sydney Markets
> Puffed-up face, no shoes upon his feet
> Checked out all the rubbish tins
> Then a kind old lady gave him a bite to eat
> He'd been bashed last night in Redfern Park
> By a gang of thugs lurking in the dark
> One of these was heard to remark:
> "That old boong was once a fighter, so they say
> That boong was once a fighter, so they say,"
> And the hungry fighter faces another day,
> The Hungry Fighter faces another day.
>
> *The Hungry Fighter* (last verse)

Aboriginal cricketer Eddy Gilbert was considered by Don Bradman to be the fastest bowler he ever faced, but Gilbert encountered huge social problems in his brief cricket career, and died in an asylum.

What is it about Aboriginals that gives them the mechanical skills that allow them to play ball games on a telepathic level? The Ella brothers, Mark, Gary and Glen played Rugby Union as though they were Cockney spivs demonstrating the pea and thimble game. They created magic, sleight-of-hand, passing the ball as though they read each other's minds. The Krakeour brothers, Phil and Jim, did the same sorts of things playing Australian Rules football. People tend to confer on Aboriginals some sixth sense, some 'peripheral vision', something in their physiology that gives them attributes not available to others.

The acquired skills probably derived from the fact that the Ellas and Krakeours were physical brothers, who understood each other's every move. Aboriginal children are usually reared in some sort of community environment, often as a result of institutionalism, benign or otherwise. Usually they live in temperate climates. Invariably they have much leisure time together. More often than not they are poor. Generally, their parents don't inhibit them: "Let them run, jump, climb," they say, on the basis that one learns by experience. "If you get cut from a sharp knife you will know how to handle it next time". Some so-called experts call that sloppy parenting, others see it as the best way for children to learn. The games played by Aboriginal kids are vigorous, simple, to the point, with minimal facilities. There's no magic to it: they simply put in more time acquiring greater mechanical skills at an earlier level. Later in life they have to contend with inhibiting, sometimes lethal social factors.

The Tiger & The Don

When I was a kid each summer meant
Long days at the MCG
With my dear old Dad, and his Gladstone bag
And his thermos of sweet, black tea
Sandwiches, and fruit cake,
Sitting up in the stand
With my Dad and his mates at the cricket,
I tell you, it was grand.

There'd be a big post mortem
As every wicket fell,
They'd pick their 'greatest ever' teams
And they wove me in their spell.
They'd argue, but there was one point
They all agreed upon
There'd never be a pair to match
The Tiger and The Don

CHORUS
My Dad said: "Feast your eyes upon
The Tiger and The Don,
You'll never see a pair like them again.
Don's the greatest bat of all
And when The Tiger's got the ball
He puts the fear of God
In all those Englishmen".

They told me of The Tiger's skills
And how there was no doubt,
Batsmen from all around the world
Could never work him out.
Arms like pistons, charges in,
Murder in his eye,
I watched The Tiger's fearsome style
And I understood just why.

He was a giant of a man
And he bowled at medium pace,
But they were spinners, mate,
They went all ways, or fizzed up at your face
A wrong'un that you'd never pick
And if that's not enough
The type of killer instinct
That would call the devil's bluff.

CHORUS

Oh, yes, feast your eyes upon
The Tiger and The Don etc

And oh, the thrill, I can feel it still
When The Don walked in to bat
He'd look around, take his block
Then he'd knock the bowlers flat.
Scorching drives, a hook, a pull,
A cut, a daring glance,
Don's policy was never to give
The bowlers any chance.

Down the pitch he'd dance
To smash the spinners off their length.
He'd hook the quickies' bumpers
And you marvelled at his strength
An eye just like an eagle's
His fame will linger on
For there'll never be a batsman
To match the Mighty Don.

CHORUS

Yes, feast your eyes upon
The Tiger and The Don
You'll never see a pair like them again.
Don's the greatest bat of all
And when The Tiger's got the ball
He puts the fear of God
In all those Englishmen.

*Logged off: forestry in remote parts of Tasmania
has been subjected to environmental protest*
Photo: Frank Hurley. By permission of the National Library of Australia

CHAPTER 22

Try To Understand

> "Try to understand, this land Australia,
> Take her as she is, her moods, her mysteries,
> Mother of us all, beneath The Southern Cross,
> In her frame of peaceful seas."
>
> Ted Egan, *This Land Australia*

There has always been an admirable pioneering spirit in Australia, and a commendable egalitarian outlook among its people. There is a worthy adherence in all things to the sporting notion of 'Have a go'. Especially in bush situations Australians have been remarkably resourceful. If something goes wrong, you fix it. The cameraderie of the frontier has always been vital and influenced in a benign way by strong family values, mateship, the writings of literary figures like 'Banjo' Paterson and Henry Lawson and, in earlier times especially, militant unionism. Australia's shearers, drovers, mariners, pastoral and agricultural workers, miners, railway construction workers and road builders, raised families and worked hard and efficiently in tough conditions. The people who settled on farms and station properties, and set up essential business enterprises in rural regions, showed immense courage and enterprise. Australia's aviators from the 1920s to the 1950s performed astonishing pioneering feats that opened up the vast inland regions, connected Australia internationally, and established unique, resourceful outback passenger and mail services. The admirable Royal Flying Doctor Service and the School of the Air were introduced. With the combination of aeroplanes, motor cars, wireless communication and imaginative people, the outback was secured.

Today the rural traditions survive, even in the crowded capital cities, notwithstanding the tremendous cultural changes also incorporated into the Australian lifestyle as a result of migration. The 'fair dinkum Aussie' role is quickly adopted by impressive numbers of newcomers. The 'dole bludgers' and the 'shirkers' are present, but in a minority. There is a healthy, pragmatic attitude to hard work among the majority of Australian people, wherever they live. That allows leisure activities to predominate and be a right, not a privilege. This is a nation well-served in terms of effective communications, fair working conditions, and a strong welfare system to cater for the unfortunate, the addicted, the afflicted, the disabled and the needy. There are always big problems, but there is always a commendable determination to resolve these.

At the important Federal level, the general quality of politicians and performance has been poor, aggravated by unilateral party politics, short electoral terms, and the consequent but sheer lack of any good, long-range planning in the national interest. Members of the federal House of Representatives are elected for three year terms. Even within that short period, the flexible system allows those in power to call elections at opportune times. Federal parliamentarians seem to spend the first of their three years paying for political favours that secured their election, the second year implementing tough budgets and cost-cutting, allowing a third year of 'pork-barrelling' to ensure re-election. Despite the admirable presence of bodies like the Council for Scientific and Industrial Research (CSIRO) that provides the wherewithal, there is no long-term planning of consequence by successive governments, for the politicians do not see the need for effective and meaningful strategies that transcend party politics. It's all too hard. There isn't time for planning. Politics is only about point-scoring. The future does not extend beyond the oft-repeated adage that 'a week is a long time in politics'.

Politicians in Australia have traditionally given an inordinate level of attention to the interests of primary producers. This is understandable, given that the wealth of Australia in the years from 1820 to 1960 was in the hands of people with strong rural interests and political clout. The influence of the minority Country Party became excessive. Of course, the wealth of the nation in that period derived from wheat and wool, and the export of other primary produce, particularly to Mother England. It must also be acknowledged that the best Australian farmers and graziers are equal to their counterparts in any part of the world.

From the 1960s Australia had to establish new markets, particularly in Asia, as a result of Britain's entry into the European Union, for that move led to a virtual abandonment of Commonwealth suppliers, particularly Australia and New Zealand. Australia found that Asia was a much more fickle market for grains, horticulture and other foodstuffs. Wool had soaring 'highs' but abysmal 'lows', and was not the guaranteed winner of previous halcyon times. Meat was often too expensive, or not to the taste of Asians. The United States and Canada proved to be attractive markets, but they were tough countries prepared at all times to subsidise their own farmers, and to impose at whim seemingly inordinate laws, conditions and excises on imported foodstuffs.

Where's the beef?: Giant road trains move cattle across thousands of miles
Photo: Hans Boessem

Japan became Australia's biggest customer, mainly for unrefined minerals. Iron ore and coal are available in abundance in Australia, and huge ships constantly ply from ports in Western Australia and Queensland. Complacent Australia then buys cars, electronic goods and white goods like refrigerators and washing machines from Japan and other Asian countries. The obvious step would be to industrialise her own north, where all the raw materials could be brought together and utilised to maximum advantage.

One of Australia's biggest present day problems derives from the past, which saw the almost criminal ineptitude of governments and landholders pursuing a policy of taking up as much land as possible for farming and grazing. Rather than confront the post World War employment issues, Australia made available large acreages of marginal land to ex-servicemen who became instant farmers on what were called 'soldier settler' blocks. Many starved. Most of those who survived did so on the basis of absolute ingenuity and hard work. In the process, the fragile land was cleared to the point where now it is endangered through salination and erosion. Yet it is still exploited by farmers and graziers who do not hesitate to demand assistance from governments every time there is a crisis. It is a safe bet that one of three devastating factors - fire, flood or drought - will prevail in substantial areas of Australia every two years. And everybody acts as though it is happening for the first time.

Every five years in Australia there are claims that the country is experiencing 'the worst drought in the last 100 years'. Unfortunately, the statement is always accurate. The droughts will go on getting worse, for the simple reason that Australia will continue to be a dry country; and the land cannot be returned to previous levels of productivity. At the height of droughts it is still common to see thousands of hungry sheep searching every inch of the barren landscape for even a blade of grass. Farmers are provided with taxpayer-funded drought relief incentives, usually in the form of interest free E.C. (Exceptional Circumstances) loans, to enable them to buy hay to feed stock in dry times, and then to purchase new stock once the drought has broken. The problem is that the hard-footed stock - cattle, sheep and horses - have in the meantime been creating havoc with the denuded landscape. Winds and eventual rains either blow or wash the topsoil away into watercourses, creeks and rivers that become silted up and are themselves reduced in stature. Rivers once plied by paddle-steamers are reduced to stagnant mudholes full of algae. It is crazy. Yet there are still cries of 'Rain follows the plough'. When New Zealand experiences red skies as a result of Australia's dust storms, as occurred in 2003, it is time for action.

People tend to say: "It's either a feast or a famine" in Australia, because droughts are often followed by flooding. And more E.C. claims. The huge problem is that settlement, farming and grazing has been undertaken without due regard to water levels of rivers, creeks, even watercourses.

What is needed is a co-ordinated policy to discourage farmers in the truly marginal or vulnerable areas from continuing the farce. Some formula like 'three doses of E.C. government assistance and you are out'. Beyond that, it can not be claimed to be bad luck: it is a bad system. Put the tree-planters in and forget the stock and crops. This is too fragile a land.

Australia is a big country, blessed with huge forest areas. Much of this is eucalypt (gum tree) country, with the trees having minimal commercial value as timber for building or furniture. In 1788 there were impressive 'old growth' forests of more exotic trees - especially cedars and native pines - along the lush coastal fringe of New South Wales, Victoria and Queensland, on the seaward side of the Great Dividing Range. In the bottom southwest corner of Western Australia there were thousands of square miles covered by huge karri, marri, and the beautiful red-blooded jarrah trees. Along the bigger rivers throughout Australia there was redgum in abundance. In Tasmania, the island state, there were magnificent forests of celery top, myrtle, blackwood, and the amazing and bountiful Huon pine - flexible, pliable, termite resistant, the most-prized timber of boat builders.

Go to any show day in any Australian country town, and you will see the world's finest axemen displaying their incredible skill in chopping and sawing logs. It is all very admirable, and arguably the best action of a show day. But it is also a reminder that in the 19th Century Australia went into a frenzy of denuding these priceless, peerless, ancient forests as a symbol of clearing or conquering the land. The streets of London and many other world cities have jarrah blocks as a base for the bitumen surface. Redgum and jarrah sleepers were provided for railways in Australia and all over the world. The biggest trees of all, the karri of Western Australia, are still being cut. If the timber was of any commercial use, it could be argued that the exploitation of trees of such awesome size has some value or meaning. But the sawn karri timber is virtually worthless, and usually is cut into stakes on which to grow tomatoes. It is difficult to find a cedar tree of any size in Australian rainforests today. The Tasmanian forests were devastated in earlier times, especially on the west coast where big mines swallowed up millions of trees for timbering underground tunnels, powering steam engines, erecting buildings and, of course, domestic firewood. The Australian logging experience has been an abysmal and total disaster. And today there are chainsaws, huge earth-moving equipment, and giant logging trucks to make the exploitation easier.

Fortunately, there is some emerging sense in the debate on forests. The Greens have increasing political appeal to many concerned environmentalists. Unions, logging companies and governments are at least talking, but there is always friction between the 'tree huggers' who want no logging, and those at the other end of the spectrum who ask cryptically: "And how do you intend to wipe your arse?" There must be middle ground established so that the number of trees planted always far exceeds the number of those cut. The mindless exploitation of old growth forests, especially the precious trees, must cease. For beauty's sake, if for no other reason.

But what of wood chipping of the plentiful eucalypts? They are suitable for paper manufacture but not much else in exploitative terms. Part of the ongoing strategy on how to come to terms with fires, particularly in settled areas of the country, should include sensible harvesting of eucalypt trees by wood chipping, on a managed grid basis, as a means of containing the annual devastation by fire of entire forests. The problem for today's householders, and wild and domestic animals, is that settlement introduces fences that hinder firefighters and trap animals in the fire season, which is every summer in eucalypt-covered Australia.

Bush fire is a misleading term. In much of inland Australia, in the more arid areas, there are fires through the bush each summer that often have some regenerative value. They can correctly be called bush fires. The trees are stunted, the fires move slowly and are relatively easy to bring under control. They can often be contained with graders and back-burning.

Then there are grass fires that destroy crops that are ripe and ready for harvest in summer. These are devastating, a total threat, for an entire livelihood can be blasted away in hours on the searing, windy, scorching days when one can smell disaster in the air. Firebreaks and the vigilance and devotion to duty of the admirable volunteer fire crews are the only defence against regional disaster each summer in the farming areas.

Much more frightening and life-threatening are the fires that sweep through the big eucalypt forests in the Great Dividing Range and along the coastal strip of eastern and southern Australia. In those regions a fire becomes a tree fire with the principal danger the unpredictability of the fire in the treetops. Given the flammable nature of gumtrees it is not uncommon, on a hot windy day, for a fire to race through miles of country in minutes. Fireballs are created, fuelled by the eucalyptus oil, and the attendant danger to human life, households and stock is horrible to contemplate and even worse to behold.

It is often said, in respect of fires, that Australia should learn from its Aboriginals. There is some truth in this as a means of handling bush fires, and, to a lesser extent, tree fires. The traditional First Australian method of controlling overgrowth in the undergrowth was to patch burn the country. It was done on a calculated basis, taking winds, temperatures and other factors into consideration. There seems no doubt that in winter months there must be patch burning, and (dare one say it) some discreet logging of eucalypts, and the planting of some foreign, less flammable trees in those areas of Australia's more sought-after suburbs, for example, the north shore of Sydney. Here people delight in having a bush view and being able to marvel at the kookaburras, the magpies, the smaller bird life, and the many colourful parrots that inhabit the eucalypt trees. The alternative to selective logging is to have worsening threats of devastating, relentless, uncontrollable, life-devouring fires. No trees. No birdlife. No houses. Dead people. Dead animals.

Transport in Australia is good, given the comparatively sparse population and the prohibitive distances involved. It is the safest country in the world for aviation. The railway network established in the late 1800s was truly amazing. The various government departments of railways were Australia's biggest employers from the 1850s to 1950s. There were navvies creating the railway lines, 'snake charmers' (fettlers) maintaining them, but also hundreds of other categories of employment that made the railway station the hub of activity for country towns. There were, for example, undertakers working on funeral trains, mail sorters working on the country mail trains handling letters addressed like this:

>Long Johnny
>Droving Conroy's Sheep
>Along the Castlereagh.

The states, that were then colonies, all established effective rail communication with even their most remote towns, but they made the colossal blunder, in jealous pre-Federation days, of implementing different rail gauges for different states. Crossing the border became a nightmare for passengers and freighters alike. Nonetheless, the continent was criss-crossed with railways, and there was a certain level of comfort provided in the knowledge that the railway was there. It was state-owned and thus predictable, if somewhat inefficient. Grain crops were harvested, stored in silos and transported by train at the whim of the various government boards that organised overseas and local markets. Cattle and sheep were taken to market in the care of train drovers. In the land of 'wait a while', people accepted that the train might be a bit late, but it would get there. Fares were manageable and the company of other passengers was often stimulating. Card games, sing-songs, book reading and refreshment rooms - 'a pie and a cuppa at the triple R' (railway refreshment rooms) - became part of the romantic railway ethos of Australia.

With characteristic lack of foresight, latter-day governments allowed railway systems to run into disrepair, to the point where it became more viable to take the easy option of more motor cars, coaches and trucks on the roads. Governments still extort obscene levels of taxation for vehicle registration, petrol and diesoline; perhaps they had a hidden agenda as the government rail services deteriorated and motor vehicles took over. Eventually the only course to follow was to discontinue much of the rail service. Rural Australia might have expected the wonderful rail infrastructure to be enhanced and electrified, to provide fast, environmentally-friendly, safe traffic for people and goods. What happened? Rail services were stopped, lines were dismantled, beautiful old railway stations fell into disrepair or were sold, thousands of rural railway workers were made redundant, and towns died as a result. Buses belching diesel fumes are now used to transport people from town to town; and huge semi-trailers and road-trains are mobile nightmares on the highways. Every adult demands a motor car: most households have two or three.

The age of the train: Australia's vast, flat outback makes rail development logical
Photo: Hans Boessem

Horsepower: today helicopters as well as horses and motor bikes are used for mustering stock on big outback stations
Photo: Hans Boessem

On the other hand, there has been a commendable concentration on upgrading arterial roads and motorways, particularly in the smaller and more heavily-populated states (where the votes are). Road travel between capital cities of Australia is now a pleasant experience. The roads are good, and regional towns, motels and roadhouses are providing excellent service and amenities for travellers. Australian truckies are usually expert, safe, considerate drivers. Given increasing demands, there must be a speedy, efficient transport system based on co-ordinated road and rail. Thus there should be a complete revitalisation of the rail system, cutting out the truly redundant lines, but putting back into place the priority of an efficient rural rail service.

Despite the rural nostalgia of Australians, it is somewhat alarming that the population in the capital cities continues to rise, while once-stable, productive country towns are dying. Fine homes, shops and public buildings are vacant in regional Australia. Australia's craziest statistic is that 90 percent of the country's population of 20 million people live in the eight capital cities, covering land area of about three percent of the nation. Not even the insane real estate prices seem to deter people from herding into the cities. Even though every move in a city like Sydney requires the traveller to allow at least one hour, people can not get enough of city life. Pollution is rife. Crime horrifies. Traffic accident statistics are atrocious. Is there no end to this frenzy?

There must be some means whereby governments can curb the growth of cities. There should certainly be bigger tax incentives and support for any business that develops and operates in areas other than capital cities. The international markets for Australia are to the north, yet the majority of Australia's people live in the more temperate, southern regions.

Perhaps there should be an incentive scheme to industrialise the north? It is fairly straightforward. Establish Tennant Creek (NT) as the point where three railways meet - the Adelaide-Alice Springs-Darwin track (completed 2004); a grain, cotton and wool express from Melbourne to Darwin via Bourke (NSW); and another obvious new track from the Pilbara region of Western Australia to Mt Isa in Queensland. That would interconnect all the huge mineral resources of inland Australia, and provide logical access to Asian markets through the port of Darwin. Water should be piped from Kimberley and Gulf of Carpentaria rivers that presently flow into the sea, and stored. Re-locate one million people, either migrants or adventurous people from other parts of Australia, give them tax incentives to live in the more difficult north, and let them build the towns, factories and steelworks that will enable Australia to become the industrial giant it should be.

The high populations of capital cities give rise every summer to the crucial question of water shortage. Most summers see the introduction of strict water restrictions for domestic gardens. Particularly in Victoria and Western Australia, water supply for their capital cities, Melbourne and Perth respectively, is often a major electoral issue.

The lack of long-term government planning is nowhere more evident than in water storage and usage. Conservationists say that Australia must not repeat exercises like the Snowy Mountains scheme, which in the 1950s turned rivers backward and enabled water storage and a massive hydro-electric system. It was hailed, in its post World War II creation days, as a miracle to transform the inland, but is vilified nowadays as the start of the degradation of the re-routed rivers. But given the ongoing population growth of capital cities, where does the required water come from? Australia is a big, dry country, with long hot summers that dry up surface water at an astonishing rate through sheer evaporation. The country is full of farmers and potential farmers who demand more and more water for rice, cotton, sugar, sorghum, anything. The rivers are flogged. The major inland rivers - the once-mighty Murray, the Murrumbidgee, the Darling, the Lachlan, the Wimmera - are all abused by locks and dams and silted as a result of over-clearing along their banks. In some cases, they have been drained to a muddy trickle through mindless irrigation of water bled from the rivers in wasteful, open-earth drains. What value rice as a crop, if it takes 1,000 litres of water to produce a cupful?

There are huge underground water supplies in the Great Artesian Basin, but that resource is not going to get larger, and much of the water drawn presently from that source is wasted in bore drains and earth irrigation channels. The big-scale damming of rivers, once considered obvious, is now frowned upon, and the dams might not be filled even if built.

There is the heartening fact that, while southern regions of Australia are hot and dry from October to March, the tropical north enjoys a monsoonal wet season in the same timespan. For many years people like writer Ion Idriess and First Australian pastoralist-cum-politician Ernie Bridge have been advocating the piping of water from the north to the south of the continent. Certainly some piping and storage of water in inland Australia must be contemplated.

In the years since Federation, Australia has established itself as a conservative western country, generally uneasy about its geographic position in Asia. Once an integral part of the British Empire, and thereby bound to follow England to the end of the earth in all matters, Australia is now held by many to be much too subordinate to the United States, in the hope that trade will be enhanced. The United States is fiercely protective of its own primary producers, so Australia's sycophantic attitude does not seem warranted on trade grounds.

Australia has good reason to align with the United States in defence matters. In entering the Pacific War against Japan post-Pearl Harbour, the Americans were acting in their own interests, but there is no doubt that it was the subsequent American presence in the Pacific, together with the heroism of Australian troops (many of them untrained boys), that saved Australia from subjugation. Having averted the prospect of slavery under Japan, Australia is justified in maintaining an uncompromising stance about its future defence.

At the same time it is interesting to note that Australia's connections, first with Britain and then with the United States, have taken this country into more wars that any other nation on earth, including Britain and America themselves. Writing in *The Australian* in April 2003, Phillip Adams refers to it as "the accumulation of Frequent Fighter Points". Australians fought for Britain in the Sudan, Khartoum, the Boer War, the two World Wars, and the campaigns in Malaya and Borneo in the 'Konfrontasi' period of the 1950s, when Prime Minister Robert Menzies assured the nation there was a Communist under every bed.

With the United States as its leader and partner, Australia sent troops to Korea, Vietnam, Kuwait, East Timor, Afghanistan and Iraq. Because of the fearsome record established by its troops during all of those campaigns, Australian soldiers are always sought for United Nations peacekeeping exercises in the Balkans, Bougainville or Africa. Australia seems exuberant about war, seems to prefer to be aggressive rather than conciliatory. It is a stance that will be difficult to maintain, given the country's determination to keep its population down. There will always be the requirement to follow a big powerful ally. Subordination to the interests of the major protagonist is inevitable; that leads to the very distasteful practice of 'arse-licking' abhorred by Australians generally. It is interesting to compare Australia's aggressive record with Commonwealth cousins, Canada and New Zealand. They, too, went all-the-way with Mother England, but they do not see the need to align with the United States now. They seem determined not to.

Australia was very easy to govern on a national basis while the country enjoyed the protection of the British Empire, and while Australian citizens were happy to call themselves British subjects. From Federation to World War II, Australia simply had to keep sending wheat, wool, meat, fruit and dairy products to Britain, and everything else fell into place. Most Australians treasured the dream of one day having the chance to 'go home' to see Mother England. A series of sound, safe, avuncular prime ministers operated on a secure, leisurely basis. This was mainly because as an island continent in a temperate region, Australia was so well-endowed that even the poor and unemployed could be warm, and eat well. The important mateship ethos was always alive and well, inspired by the great Australian poets.

Prime Minister John Curtin meets U.S. General Douglas MacArthur in Melbourne in 1942

It was not until World War II that an Australian prime minister was forced to enter the world stage. Labor leader John Curtin confronted and angered British Prime Minister Winston Churchill and the British Government as he ordered the Australian troops home from fighting Allied battles to defend this nation against Japan. Alliances with the United States were sought, and achieved. Curtin and his Australian Labor Party (ALP) successor, Ben Chifley, will always be remembered as great prime ministers, because they took Australia to independence, and performed admirably through the war and during the impressive years of post-war reconstruction.

Liberal Prime Minister Robert Menzies is revered in conservative political circles, and was also admired, if begrudgingly, by his ALP opponents. Menzies was fortunate to be in power in a peaceful period when jobs were plentiful, and wool and wheat created wealth. The Anglophile Australian Prime Minister became a much respected figure within the powerful British Commonwealth. Most Australians felt safe with Menzies at the helm from 1949 to 1964.

Post-Menzies, there was a succession of Liberal prime ministers, Holt, Gorton and McMahon, who ranged from the inept to the ludicrous. In 1972 the Australian Labor Party returned to power with Gough Whitlam as its leader after 23 years in opposition. Whitlam swept the board clean. He strode onto the world stage, flamboyant, sometimes magnificent. He took Australia out of the Vietnam War, recognised China as a world force, and introduced huge social reform, including the establishment of a Family Court, and Medibank, a comprehensive National Health scheme. He sought a better deal for the First Australians. At the same time he was like a drunk in a brewery, as he allowed his inexperienced Cabinet ministers to create mayhem with the economy. And Whitlam's ego was bigger than the huge man himself.

The conservative bodies that are the real power-brokers of Australia, aided by the subversive infiltration of United States agencies, helped to set up the scenario whereby Whitlam was dismissed from office, in 1975, by the Governor-General, Sir John Kerr. Kerr implemented imperial powers on behalf of the Australian Head of State, Queen Elizabeth, in an action that must have made Whitehall squirm. Whitlam was gone, but will never be forgotten.

He was succeeded by Malcolm Fraser, a patrician farmer-cum-politician who would, many years later, do an impressive *volte face* in social matters, but who as a prime minister was pedestrian and cautious, keen mainly to put the Whitlam reforms aside. In Fraser's defence, it must be said that he was determined to continue to seek better conditions for Aboriginals. It was he who kept the Whitlam enterprise going in that area. The first land rights legislation was introduced by Fraser.

After Fraser came a 20-year period of quite impressive national government, with three very different prime ministers. Labor's Bob Hawke and Paul Keating led the country from 1983 to 1996. On 2 March 1996, Liberal leader John Howard defeated Keating. What is interesting is that these three leaders all seemed to understand, in their very different ways, that Australia could not be insular. The best possible world position must be sought. Their tactics varied. Hawke and Keating were suspicious of the United States (as indeed was the US of them) but relaxed in Asia and Oceania, easily wearing the mandatory flamboyant shirts at the various conferences. They were aloof towards Britain. By contrast, Howard was totally out of place in the shirts, but easy, confident and relaxed among the suits in Washington and London. Although lampooned by Australian cartoonists as a lap-dog and puppet of the United States, Howard's Australian electoral support, his survival within his own party, and his achievements in trade deals with the United States, are evidence of considerable political ability.

The most radical free-market reforms in Australian history were implemented by Hawke, with Keating as his treasurer. In a series of actions that would have horrified his socialist mentor Ben Chifley, Hawke - of all things, a former leader of the Australian Council of Trade Unions - floated the dollar, abandoned centralised wage-fixing, and sold the Commonwealth Bank and the national airline, Qantas. Tariffs were slashed, and the inordinate influence of the Country Party was gone forever. Trade with Asia boomed.

Keating, Hawke's successor as prime minister, probably read the international picture better than anybody. Keating was an enigma. Compassionate, emotional, articulate, shy yet acid-tongued, intelligent to an awesome level, he was particularly impressive in international politics, even if he did read President Suharto of Indonesia inaccurately. Keating had problems because of a driving ego, an intolerance of fools, and a lack of people skills. "Get a job" he snarled at a critic. His political opponents grabbed the moment, and the TV footage. The next electoral campaign was won and lost around the statement and Keating's apparent uncaring attitude.

The future should be brighter. Aboriginal girls at Yirara College, Alice Springs.
Photo Carmel Sears.

Howard, who had been Fraser's stodgy, unadventurous treasurer, became a consummate politician as prime minister. He presented a dull but safe, caring visage to most people. In times of national need, bushfires, floods, the 2002 Bali bombings, the Iraq War, he was Johnny-on-the-spot. Like Menzies, he presented - almost imposed himself - as something of a doyen among cricketers. He continued economic reform, and introduced and maintained tough criteria for all welfare recipients. He and his willing Cabinet colleagues engaged in hefty trade-union bashing, a sure tactic to win votes in conservative Australia. He deftly won an election with an unlikely prize to voters - the introduction of a Goods and Services Tax! Australia has never seen political sleight-of-hand to match it. His uncanny ability to read the electorate enabled Howard to take inflexible stances on gun reform, republican issues, immigration and entry into the Iraq War. In every case he read the voters correctly. Howard received great support from an adroit treasurer, Peter Costello. The economy has thrived, there are free trade agreements with the United States, trade surpluses aided by effective marketing, and burgeoning Australian export industries, for example in wine sales. Howard has been hard-nosed on welfare and arrogant in Aboriginal Affairs, probably on the undeniable if sad grounds that there are no positive votes in blackfellow issues. For all the above reasons John Howard will perhaps be remembered, in populist, affluent, conservative circles, as Australia's best-ever prime minister. Deeper-thinking people may have other preferences.

Howard's political fortunes have been enhanced by the awful facts of fear and conflict. The prime minister was unequivocal in his support of the US and Britain in Iraq. Victory was swift and efficient: Australian troops were awesome. John Howard said farewell to them, and welcomed them back. The world is now doomed to ongoing terrorist threats. Of course nobody condones incidents like the 2002 Bali bombings, but it is easy for a leader to look good while promising Churchillian reprisal as he walks through the ashes, consoling relatives and survivors, and pinning bravery medals on heroes like football star Jason McCartney, who saved lives at Bali with contemporary 'Man with the Donkey' courage. To Howard's credit, he reads such situations with intrinsic, genuine compassion as well as immense political awareness. He knows that nothing else really matters if lives and lifestyle are in jeopardy. Johnny-on-the-spot. A clever fellow.

Willy The Whingeing Pom

I'm Willy the Whingeing Pom,
Guess where I come from?
I went 'Down Under' from the old UK
But I much prefer the British way
Rule Britannia
I'm Willy the Whingeing Pom.

I heard about Orstralia
From a man down in The Strand
How things was a terrible failure
In that far-off southern land
Sez he: "Australia's in a mess,
They need a chap like you
So they can solve their problems, mate
And learn a trick or two".

The plane trip out was dreadful
Do you know what the Aussies did?
Even though I was goin' to save 'em
I had to pay ten bloomin' quid.
And when I arrived in Sydney
No red carpet did I see
Just a mob of Aussies shoutin' out
"Go home, you Pommy B————"

And they were talkin' to -
CHORUS : Willy the Whingeing Pom etc

Well, now I'm in Orstralia
I think it's right and fittin'
That I got the job to teach this mob
How we do things back in Britain
But they won't line up to catch the bus
No queues to use the Loos
The Aussies out in public
Are as wild as kangaroos
(When they're on the booze)

The beaches aren't like Blackpool
You can't buy Jellied Eel
And they have trouble recognising
My British sex appeal
Cos they laugh when I go walking
In me sandals and me sox
Me suit from Saville Row, you know
Me Marks and Spencer's jocks.

In conclusion I'll just say
It's nothing like back home
And sometimes I'm regretful
That I started out to roam.
But I'll stay and I'll have a giggle
As I civilise this 'ere lot
And I'll have me bath each Saturday night
Wevver I need it or not!

Because I'm:
CHORUS   Willy the Whingeing Pom etc

I've Been Everywhere, Ma'am

I was 'humpin' me Bluey'
On the dusty Oodnadatta Track
When along comes a tourist lady
Headin' for The Great Outback
So I thumbs her down and asks her:
"Any chance of a ride?"
She looks at me - excited like,
And beckons me inside.
She asks me if I've seen a road
With so much dust and sand.
I said : "Listen, lady, I've travelled
Every road in this 'ere land".

CHORUS

Cos, I've been everywhere, Ma'am
I've been everywhere, Ma'am
Breathed the mountain air, Ma'am
Crossed the desert spare, Ma'am
Trouble I've had my share, Ma'am
I've been everywhere."

I've been to Paratta, Coolangatta,
Parramatta, Karrakatta,
Tallangatta, Wangaratta, Cabramatta,
Oodnadatta,
Turramurra, Burramurra, Kununurra,
Muttaburra,
Minamurra, Tibooburra, Murrumburra,
Yungaburra

CHORUS
I've been everywhere etc

I've been to Milla Milla, Bogabilla,
Kangarilla, Wallumbilla,
Yankalilla, Mundrabilla, Cowandilla,
Marawilla,
Uralla, Augathella, Brindabella, Wanganella
Sarsparilla, Yirrkala, Eumeralla, I'm the
feller

CHORUS
I've been everywhere etc

I've been to Wungong, Cunjerong, Jigalong,
Mittagong,
Kongorong, Tuggeranong, Grong Grong,
Derriwong,
Illawong, Jugiong, Koolatong, Wollongong,
Binalong, Kurrajong, Ettawong, Euabalong

CHORUS
I've been everywhere, Ma'am etc

I've been to Dandalup, Karrinyup,
Joondalup, Porongerup,
Kundinup, Dwellingup, Yalingup,
Gnowangerup,
Yunderup, Nockerup, Balingup, Manjimup,
Cookernup, Mumbleup, Kojonup, so "Fill
em up"

CHORUS
I've been everywhere, Ma'am etc

Ten pound passengers: the arrival of migrants from Europe
By permission of the Government Printing Office collection, State Library of New South Wales

CHAPTER 23

Not Alien, Australian

> We are one, we are many
> And from all the lands of the world we come
> We share our dream, we sing with one voice
> I am, you are, we are Australian
>
> Bruce Woodley, Dobe Newton, *I Am Australian*

By any standards, the Australia of the 21st century is an attractive and stable country. Its economy is sound. It is multi-cultural. It is also a hi-tech country, belying its earlier times when it lived off the farm. It is still a granary and the world's great quarry, but it is well to the fore in important areas like optics, biotechnology and other sciences. Tertiary education is a major export earner, as is tourism. Australia also is in the top five of countries in the use of the internet.

Perhaps as important, it is now seen by most Asian countries as part of their region, neutral ground where they can meet and do business. The British connection remains strong, but mostly through family reunions, tourism and sporting events. Australia remains an ally of the United States, because it needs the protection of the world's only superpower.

Two hundred years after the convicts arrived, involuntarily, there are now many who would chose to follow their trail. But today, migration to Australia is not easy. Generally race is not a factor. Annual quotas are set, and points are allocated in various categories to establish suitability. Family reunification is possible, but strenuously checked. 'Boat people', once tolerated as refugees, are turned away whenever possible on the grounds that they are 'queue jumpers'. Those who have achieved access to Australia on various precarious boats are held in barbaric detention camps - men, women and children - and subjected to inexplicable, interminable delays in processing their claims for refugee status.

The majority of Australian people and politicians endorse the continuation of these policies. Migration is, and will continue to be, Australia's hottest political issue. A stern, uncompromising interpretation of the rules of immigration almost certainly won the 2001 Federal election for Prime Minister John Howard and the Liberal National Coalition. At the same time Australia is seen by many Australians themselves, and certainly by some international critics, as being tough, arrogant, selfish, uncaring - and cynically in breach of various United Nations Conventions on refugees that have been established by signatory nations, including Australia.

Most Australians favour minimal immigration, on the grounds that unemployment is a factor of Australian life, and major cities to which migrants are attracted are over-crowded and crime-ridden. There is a selfish belief that a smaller population is desirable.

There is a tendency for new waves of migrants to set up enclaves in the various capital cities. Thus Cabramatta in Sydney and the Richmond and Collingwood areas of Melbourne are very Vietnamese. Doncaster in Melbourne is home to the majority of wealthier Hong Kong Chinese. Muslims tend to favour the western suburbs of Sydney. While, at the outset this creates problems and ethnic crime, it is totally understandable, given language, religious and socio-economic factors. It is balanced somewhat by the establishment of wonderful, exotic features like incomparable restaurants, and shops selling addictive foodstuffs and clothing.

Time and patience are required. Australia has had similar experiences in previous generations. The great Australian lifestyle will sort things out. And do we not now point with pride to earlier ghetto dwellers like the Chinese of Little Bourke Street in Melbourne and Sydney's Broadway, the Italians of Lygon Street in Carlton, and the Lebanese of Newtown, as the best representatives of multi-cultured Australia? Like New York's Jews and Irish, these are marvellous Australian examples that, given patience, integration of the best kind can be achieved.

Diversity works: Multi-cultural Council in Darwin
Photo: Department of Multi-cultural Affairs

There are occasional flashes of racial tension, and a xenophobic streak in most Australians, but people quickly feel free to defend their own position. Ugly labels such as wog, slope and coon are heard, though most people refuse to contemplate or condone usage of such offensive words. There is a commendable habit of turning these derogatory terms around. Ask the Darwin Chinese, the Melbourne Greeks, the north Queensland Italians, the Barossa Valley Germans, the West Australian Slavs, the Adelaide Latvians about squareheads, chinks and dagoes about race relations in general, and they will give you a healthy mouthful to show who knows what about Australia. As Eddy Quong, fifth generation Australian, said: "Rice, mate! I only ever had one bowl of rice, and look what happened to me eyes and me nose!" Utter a racist comment in multi-racial Darwin, and you will get a whack under the ear from the least expected quarter.

But...there is still unfortunate ignorance throughout Australia about the degree of dispossession of the First Australians. Many other Australians, pampered by their own easy, inherited lifestyle, will tell you that Aboriginals are spoilt, that 'they are given too much'. There is too often a tendency to equate money shown in government budgets, spent by ATSIC, or provided for Aboriginal welfare, as being cash in the pockets of individual Aboriginals. Try telling that to Jacky the Blackfellow living in a humpy on the edge of some fly-blown outback town. Mine tinkit he laugh.

THE END

She's Australian

She comes from Macedonia,
Lebanon, Cambodia,
El Salvador or Chile,
Perhaps she's Vietnamese?
She's working in the factory
She's bringing up her family
She's all, she's all,
She's all or any one of these.

Her clothes are somewhat different,
She doesn't speak much English,
Worships at a different church
She's never tasted beer
But she's working away relentlessly,
She's good for the economy
In every sense this woman's an Australian pioneer.

CHORUS
She's here, she's here, she's living over here
She's not an alien, she's Australian
And she's a pioneer

She's out there on the factory floor,
Legs are aching, feet are sore,
Mindless repetition,
But she hopes it's for the best
Wondering: Am I pregnant?
Can we afford another child?
Longing, longing for elusive hours of rest.

The factory whistle blows,
She quickly hurries for the bus,
Ignores the jibes and insults
Pretends she doesn't hear.
Run and do the shopping,
Cook the family's dinner,
No rest for her, this woman
This Australian pioneer

CHORUS
She's here, she's here etc

She doesn't drive a bullock wagon
Crack a stockwhip, ride a horse
But I guess if she had to
She'd quickly find a way
She's nonetheless a sister
To the women of another time
Who did those things, they surely did,
And are revered today.

She came out to Australia
From a homeland wracked with poverty
Hunger and oppression
A life of constant fear
Nonetheless it's difficult
The new life's so bewildering
And the woman's never heard
Of crazy words like 'pioneer'.

CHORUS
She's here, she's here etc

The kids are home from school
But the city's just so stifling
Remember all those dreams about
The beaches, bush and sun.
Late at night she sits awhile
Thinking of her childhood
Reflecting, reflecting
On the new life she's begun.

But her son will play for Collingwood
Her daughter's Jana Wendt
And Australia should be grateful
That she came over here
For she's working away relentlessly
She's good for the economy
She's laying the foundations
This Australian pioneer.

CHORUS
She's here, she's here etc

This Land Australia

Try to understand
This land Australia
Take her as she is
Her moods, her mysteries
Mother of us all
Beneath the Southern Cross
In her frame of peaceful seas.

The shimmer of the midday haze
On endless inland plains
The busy city's bustling pace
The drenching life-filled rains

Try to understand etc

The lustre of The Barrier Reef
The snow-clad Alps on high,
The fires, the floods, the searing droughts
Just love her, don't ask why

But try to understand etc

The tribal stories, ages old
The deeds of pioneers
The way of life we proudly hold
The triumphs and the tears

Try to understand etc

GLOSSARY OF TERMS

AFL	Australian Football League
AIF	Australian Imperial Forces - the Australian Army
ATSIC	Aboriginal and Torres Straits Islands Commission
AWL	Absent Without Leave. Called AWOL in America
AWU	Australian Workers' Union
Aboriginals Ordinance	Discriminatory law, now repealed, to cover the movements and rights of Australia's Aboriginal people
Anti-scorbutics	Foodstuffs - especially green vegetables - to prevent scurvy
Big Runs	Large pastoral properties, also called stations
Bitumen	tarred roads
Blackbirding	The kidnapping of Pacific Islanders, enslaved for work on sugar plantations in northern Australia. See *Kanakas*
Blanket Day	Each winter Aboriginals on mission stations were issued with a 'government' blanket
Bleed the generator	When a diesel engine runs out of fuel, the injectors have to be 'bled' with the new fuel to eliminate air bubbles. On some remote outback properties electric power is generated using diesel engines. Today solar power is being introduced.
Blue	Several obscure meanings. (1) A person with red (auburn) hair is often nicknamed 'Blue' in Australia. In earlier times (as with Nat Buchanan) a person with steely-grey hair was called Bluey. (2) A swag, or bedroll, is sometimes called a 'Bluey' or a Blue - "We humped our Blues serenely". (3) A fight is often referred to as a 'blue' - "He got into a fair old blue" "Don't stack on a blue"= "Don't start an argument". (4) There is a famous breed of Australian cattle dogs called Blue Heelers, and a common name for these dogs is 'Blue' or 'Bluey'.
Boy from Bowral, the	Don Bradman, the famous cricketer, was born in 1908 at Cootamundra, NSW, but his formative years were spent in Bowral, NSW
Bounty system	A system whereby agents in England were paid a bounty to recruit workers for prospective employers in Australia
Bushrangers	Armed, mounted robbers or highwaymen who travelled the bush roads in Australia

Bullocks	Castrated, older male cattle. Called steers when young - up to three years of age
Bullocky's Joy	Treacle. A "bullocky" is the person in charge of a bullock team, used on the Australian frontier to pull huge loads. A tin of treacle was often the 'bonus' given to Aboriginals on mission stations if they attended church services.
Bushies	An affectionate name, used by *bushies* themselves, to denote people who not only live in the bush: they belong there.
Bucks	Derogatory term for Aboriginal men
BYO	'Bring Your Own'. Particularly applies today to restaurants in Australia, where diners are invited to BYO Liquor
Chooks	One of the great Australian words meaning hens, fowls, chickens
CWA	Country Womens Association
CO	Commanding Officer
Cobber	Friend, mate. Probably an Aboriginal word
Cockrag	Slang term for a square metre of cloth tied like a baby's napkin, introduced by missionaries as a pubic covering for Aboriginal men and boys. More correctly called a narga
Colonial cringe	Whereby Australians think that British/European/American, i.e., Old World products, people, traditions etc are superior to Australian equivalents.
Come in, Spinner	In the game *Two-up*, the ring-keeper (the 'boxer' as he is called) calls "Come in Spinner" when all bets are laid and it is time to spin the coins. See *Two-up*
Coolies	Foreign, indentured labourers, especially Chinese and Indian. See *navvies*
Cop it	endure it, especially hardship.
Correspondence lessons	Today called Distance Education. Children in the bush receive a fortnight's lessons by mail, and these when completed are posted back to teachers at the Correspondence School. Mothers or governesses supervise. A marvellous system.
Corroborees	Dances performed by Aboriginals.
Cuppa, a	A cup of tea
Currency	A self-bestowed name, applied to people born in Australia, as opposed to *Sterling*, people born in the British Isles.

Daguragu, pronounced Dar-goo-ra-goo	The symbol of the struggle by the Gurindji tribe for their rights. Dagaragu is the Gurindji name for the place white people call Wattie Creek. Wave Hill was nearby Crown Land, on which a town called Kalkeringi was built to entice the Gurindji to abandon their land claims.
Depot	A camp established in the bush, where there is ample water and feed for stock. The personnel remain at 'the depot' until the next 'depot' is located and established
Diggers	Term used by Australian and New Zealand soldiers, in World War I, and ongoing, to refer to themselves.
Distance Education	Sometimes called School of the Air. Education of children in remote regions by teachers at a regional town base, incorporating wireless, satellites and the internet. See also *VISE* and *ICPA*
Dole bludgers	People who exploit the welfare system, particuarly in respect of unemployment benefits
Don, the	Nickname of Don Bradman, greatest batsman ever in the game of cricket. See *The Boy from Bowral*
Drovers	People in charge of mobs of cattle, sheep or horses being walked overland. See also *Overlanders*
Emancipists	Time-expired convicts
Exclusives	Former soldiers, who became - with their families - large landholders in Australia
Fair dinkum	Really true, genuine. From the Cantonese *xing kim* meaning real gold
First Australians	The Aboriginal people of Australia.
Flagon of plonk	a large bottle of low-quality, fortified wine
Frank Hardy	An activist author who helped the Gurindji.
Gins	Derogatory term for Aboriginal women
Hard-gutted	Fit, lean, warrior types.
Hags	Ugly old women. Also *harridans*
Humpies	Crude shelters made of basic material
Humping the bluey	Carrying the swag. See *swag*
ICPA	Isolated Childrens Parents Association. A very active body representing the interests of children unable (because of isolation) to attend normal schools. See *Distance Education, VISE*
Jig-jogged	Trotted, a term to denote the swift movement through the bush of Chinese miners on the way to the Australian Gooldfields.

Joey	A baby kangaroo
Joss House	Usually today called the Temple. The place of worship of Chinese people in Australia.
Kaititj	A Central Australian Aboriginal tribe
Kanakas	A derogatory term applied to kidnapped Pacific Islanders - see *Blackbirding*
Kick, out of his	Out of his pocket
Kimberley run, Fitzroy	A station named Fitzroy in the Kimberley (northwest) region of Western Australia.
Land rights	The term used in Australia in the quest to promote justice through recognition of the traditional ownership and occupancy of land by Aboriginals.
Lithgow Flash, the	Marjorie Jackson, Australian sprinter, born Lithgow (NSW) who won Gold Medals for the 100 and 200 metres at the Helsinki Olympics, 1952. Appointed Governor of South Australia in 2000.
MCG	Melbourne Cricket Ground
Mobs	When cattle and sheep are walked overland they are referred to as being in mobs, never herds.
Murranji, Murchison	Surveyed stock routes in inland Australia along which cattle came to be walked. Both were particularly treacherous, given the absence of water. They were called dry stages and cattle often had to be flogged to get them through.
Navvies	Menial labourers, but *not* foreigners. See *coolies*
New chums	New arrivals in Australia, especially from Britain
Night horses	Sure-footed, reliable horses tied up at night in case cattle 'rushed'
Old Dart	England
Overlanders	People who initially took stock - cattle, sheep and horses - to establish *Stations* in remote regions of Australia. See also *Drovers*
Pom/Poms/Pommy	Slang for English. Either noun or adjective. Derives from **P**roducts **O**f **M**other **E**ngland.
Pork-barrelling	Inordinate bestowal of favours, especially when politicians hand out taxpayers money to win votes
Recidivists	Convicts who offend again, after their original term of banishment/incarceration has expired
RFDS	Royal Flying Doctor Service. A medical service for outback people, based on the use of wireless and aeroplanes. Founded by Reverend John Flynn ('Flynn of the Inland') in 1917.

Ringbarking	Killing trees, by cutting the bark in a ring around the circumference of the trunk
Road trains	Huge - sometimes 70 metres in length - articulated motor trucks used for transporting stock and freight in outback Australia. Usually consists of a prime mover and three long 'dogs' (trailers). See illustration p.195
Rush	When cattle break away, particularly at night, during a droving trip. Australian drovers generally refuse to employ equivalent American terminology, like stampede, for such situations
Samples	Specimens of rare minerals, especially gold.
Sandgropers	The nickname given to the people of Western Australia
Scabs	A derogatory term for workers who do not join trade unions.
School of Mines	In every large mining town there was a School of Mines, a combination of museum, assay office, registry
Sheilas	Girls
Shelly	A frontier adjective, used to describe cattle in very poor condition
Shinplasters	In frontier days, people often issued their own 'money'. For safe-keeping these 'notes' were often inserted by bushmen in their socks, as today's athletes wear shinguards.
Sledging	Especially in cricket, the practice of abusing the opposition players.
Southern Cross	The constellation *Crux Australis*, most prominent stars in the Southern Hemisphere, featured on the Australian flag.
Squatters/squattocracy	Derogatory term for large landholders.
Station	A large grazing property. Not a farm. The equivalent of the North American term ranch, but stations in Australia are never small. If the property is small, it is a farm.
Station hands	Workers on cattle and sheep stations
Sterling	The name given to early British free settlers in Australia, as distinct from convicts. See also *Currency*.
Stud	Derogatory term for Aboriginal women who were kidnapped and sexually exploited.
Swag	Bedroll carried by itinerant workers in outback Australia. Usually consists of a canvas sheet, in which are rolled blanket(s) and spare clothing. Also called *bluey* or *drum*. He carried his swag means he humped his bluey.

Tail the horses	Assemble the horses. At night, on droving trips, horses were put out to graze, usually with hobbles on their front feet. It was the job of the 'horse tailer' to muster the horses and have them ready for the riders at daybreak. Often a bell (a 'Condamine' bell) would be placed on the necks of particular horses, to enable them to be more easily located.
Tally	The number of sheep shorn in a given day.
Thumbs her down	'Hitched' a ride in her car
Tiger, the	The nickname of Bill O'Reilly, greatest bowler ever in the game of cricket
Two-up	A game played by Australians, whereby two pennies are tossed in the air, and wagers are laid on 'heads' or 'tails'. See *Come in Spinner*
VISE	Volunteers for Isolated Students Education. A pool of retired school teachers available for short-term posting to outback emergency educational situations see *Distance Education, ICPA, Correspondence Lessons*
Wakefield System	A system of land allocation, especially in South Australia, whereby the land was sold to wealthy free settlers, and the proceeds used for the costs of transporting workers to Australia
Walers	Deriving from New South *Wales*, the generic name of the specific breed of stock horses developed in Australia. 120,000 Walers were taken by Australian soldiers to World War I. only one horse returned. See Chapter 18
Walk in, walk out	An auctioneer's term (written w.i.w.o) to denote that one party vacates, the other takes over, and all property stays in place
Whipping up water	an ingenious system, developed in inland Australia, whereby water was drawn ('whipped') from deep wells, using a beast to pull buckets operated by ropes and pulleys mounted on a headframe.
White Chinaman	Henry Lee was a very famous man in Darwin. Although Caucasian, he was reared by the Lee Family, and was a fluent speaker of Cantonese, Mandarin and Si Yip languages.
Wogs	In earlier English situations a derogatory term for Worthy Oriental Gentlemen. In Australia it is a derogatory term to describe any non-English-speaking people
Yellerfellers	A derogatory term for people of mixed-race, involving some degree of Aboriginality

RECOMMENDED READING LIST

Adam-Smith P	*The Anzacs*	Melbourne	1978
	Goodbye Girlie	Melbourne	1994
Attenborough D	*Quest Under Capricorn*	London	1963
Bain M A	*Full Fathom Five*	Perth	1982
Baker S J	*The Drum*	Sydney	1959
Barker H M	*Camels and the Outback*	Melbourne	1964
Beadell L	*Still in the Bush*	Adelaide	1975
Bean C E W	*Anzac to Amiens*	Sydney	1921
Beckett J	*A New Chum Looks at Queensland*	Ilfracombe, England	1965
Bensen I	*The Man with The Donkey*	London	1965
Blainey G	*The Tyranny of Distance*	Sydney	1966
Boldrewood R	*Robbery Under Arms*	London	1888
Bowden T	*Spooling Through*	Sydney	2003
Braddon R	*The Naked Island*	London	1961
Brennan F	*Sharing the Country*	Melbourne	1991
Buchanan G	*Packhorse and Waterhole*	Perth	1984
Buchanan Bobbie	*In the Tracks of Old Bluey*	Queensland	1994
Cahill J	*Forgotten Patriots*	Toronto	1998
Clark M	*A History of Australia*	Melbourne	1990
Clark M	*Henry Lawson: The Man and The Legend*	Melbourne	1978
Clune F	*Wild Colonial Boys*	Sydney	1948
Cole T	*Hell, West and Crooked*	Sydney	1980
Coombs H C	*Trial Balance*	Melbourne	1981
Crisp L F	*Australian National Government*	Melbourne	1965
Cusack D	*Come in Spinner*	Sydney	1951
Dark E	*Lantana Lane*	New York	1959

Davison F D	*Man Shy*	Sydney	1962
Dennis C J	*Songs of a Sentimental Bloke*	Sydney	1915
	The Moods of Ginger Mick	Sydney	1916
Devine J	*The Rats of Tobruk*	Sydney	1943
Durack M	*Kings in Grass Castles*	London	1959
Egan T	*Justice All Their Own*	Melbourne	1998
	Sitdown Up North	Sydney	1997
	The Paperboy's War	Sydney	1993
Facey A B	*A Fortunate Life*	Fremantle	1981
Fenton C	*Flying Doctor*	Melbourne	1947
Fingleton J	*Fingleton on Cricket*	London	1972
Franklin M	*My Brilliant Career*	Edinburgh	1901
Furphy J	*Such is Life*	Sydney	1903
Gammage B	*The Broken Years*	Canberra	1974
Garvey K	*Tales of My Uncle Harry*	Sydney	1978
Giles E	*Australia Twice Traversed*	London	1889
Gilmore M	*Old Days, Old Ways*	Sydney	1934
Gordon A L	*Bush Ballads and Galloping Rhymes*	Melbourne	1870
Gunn Mrs A	*We of The Never Never*	London	1908
Hardy F	*Power Without Glory*	Melbourne	1950
	The Unlucky Australians	Melbourne	1968
Harney W E	*Grief, Gaiety and Aborigines*	London	1961
	Content to Lie in the Sun	London	1958
Herbert X	*Capricornia*	Sydney	1938
	Soldiers Women	Sydney	1961
Hill E	*The Territory*	Sydney	1951
Humphries B	*Barry McKenzie*	London	1968
Hughes R	*The Fatal Shore*	London	1987

Idriess I L	*Forty Fathoms Deep*	Sydney	1937
James B	*No Man's Land*	Sydney	1989
Johnston G H	*My Brother Jack*	London	1964
Jolley E	*The Newspaper of Claremont Street*	Fremantle	1981
Keneally T	*The Playmaker*	Sydney	1990
	The Chant of Jimmy Blacksmith	Sydney	1976
Lang J T	*I Remember*	Sydney	1956
Lawler R	*The Piccadilly Bushman*	London	1961
	Summer of the 17th Doll	London	1965
Lawson H	*While the Billy Boils*	Sydney	1896
	Short Stories	Sydney	1894
	Complete Works		
Long G	*The Six Years War*	Canberra	1973
Long J P M	*The Go-Betweens*	Darwin	1992
Lowenstein W	*Weevils in the Flour*	Melbourne	1978
Lower L	*Here's Luck*	Sydney	1930
Macknight C	*Voyage to Marege*	Melbourne	1976
McGrath A	*Born in the Cattle*	Sydney	1987
McLaren J	*My Crowded Solitude*	London	1926
Markus A	*Governing Savages*	Sydney	1990
Marr D	*The High Price of Heaven*	Sydney	1999
Marshall A	*These are My People*	Melbourne	1944
Moffitt I	*The U-Jack Society*	Sydney	1972
Moorehead A	*Gallipoli*	London	1956
Morgan S	*My Place*	Perth	1988
Mulvaney D J	*Cricket Walkabout*	Melbourne	1967
Niland D	*The Shiralee*	New York	1955
	Dead Men Running	Sydney	1969

O'Brien J	*Around the Boree Log*	Sydney	1921
Ogilvie W H	*Fair Girls and Grey Horses*	Sydney	1898
O'Grady J P	*Gone Troppo*	Sydney	1968
Palmer V	*The World of Men*	Sydney	1962
Park R	*Harp in the South*	Boston	1948
	Poor Man's Orange	Sydney	1949
Pedersen H	*Jandamarra*	Broome	1995
Paterson A B	*Complete Works*	Sydney	1983
	The Old Bush Songs	Sydney	1905
Porteous R S	*Cattleman*	Sydney	1960
Porter H	*Watcher on the Cast-Iron Balcony*	London	1963
Quilty T	*The Drover's Cook*	Sydney	1958
Ratcliffe F	*Flying Fox and Drifting Sand*	New York	1938
Ronan T	*Vision Splendid*	London	1954
	Moleskin Midas	London	1956
Rowley C D	*The Destruction of Aboriginal Society*	Canberra	1970
Shute N	*A Town Like Alice*	London	1950
Simpson B F	*The Packhorse Drover*	Sydney	1990
Stuart D R	*Yandy*	Melbourne	1959
Stuart J M	*Explorations in Australia*	Adelaide	1860
Summers A	*Damned Whores and God's Police*	Melbourne	1975
Tennant K	*The Battlers*	London	1939
Thiele C	*The Sun on the Stubble*	Adelaide	1961
Warner W L	*A Black Civilisation*	New York	1958
White P	*Riders in the Chariot*	London	1961
Whitehead A	*Paradise Mislaid*	Brisbane	1997
Williams N	*Two Laws*	Canberra	1987
Williamson D	*Don's Party*	Sydney	1973
Winton T	*Cloudstreet*	Melbourne	1991